W9-ARD-925

Oklahomeland

Oklahomeland

Jeanetta Calhoun Mish

LAMAR UNIVERSITY
LITERARY PRESS

Copyright © 2015 Jeanetta Calhoun Mish
All Rights Reserved

ISBN: 978-1-942956-09-9
Library of Congress Control Number: 2015945370

For the cover and title of this book, thanks to
the anonymous graffiti artist
who painted *Oklahomeland* on a wall
in the Plaza District of Oklahoma City

Lamar University Press
Beaumont, Texas

for my Oklahomies

Recent Nonfiction from Lamar University Literary Press

Jean Andrews, *High Tides, Low Tides*
Robert Murray Davis, *Levels of Incompetence: An Academic Life*
Ted L. Estess, *Fishing Spirit Lake*
Dominique Inge, *A Garden on the Brazos*
Jim McJunkin, *Deep Sleep*
Jim Sanderson, *Sanderson's Fiction Writing Manual*

For Information on these and other books, go to
www.lamar.edu/literarypress

Acknowledgments

I am grateful to the editors of the following journals and anthologies for publishing some of the essays in this book.

Sugar Mule
> "Who/What? Oklahomans/Writing"
> "Broken Branches"

Oklahoma Today
> "Looking for (Ralph) Ellison"
> "Western Civilization"
> "Remembering Number Nine"

World Literature Today
> "A Review of Woody Guthrie's House of Earth"
> "A Review of Linda Hogan's Dark, Sweet"

Working Class Studies Newsletter
> "Two New Working-Class Poetry Collections"

Oklahoma Revelator
> " Culture Warriors: Reclaiming a Useful Term Appropriated and Abused by the Radical Right"

Landscape Dreams: A New Mexico Portrait, (UNM Press)
> "Meditative Presence: The Photographs of Craig Varjabedian"

Red Dirt Book Festival 2003 Anthology; republished in *Crosstimbers*
> "This Oklahoma We Call Home"

CONTENTS

The Arts

Oklahomeland

The Arts

Introduction & Gratitude

There are two sections in this prose collection: "The Arts" and "Oklahomeland"; the sections represent the two kinds of prose I most frequently write, that is, essays about Oklahoma and Oklahoma culture and my Oklahoma family and writings on the arts, particularly literature. Moreover, all the essays have been previously published except one, the final essay on Oklahoma's and its citizens' historical and contemporary confrontations with race and class. I'm not going to say any more about the essays—you have the book in your hand, and I trust you to read it.

As I was compiling this collection, it became clear to me that I have been the lucky recipient of many scholars' and writers' and editors' intellectual generosity; evidence of their kindnesses is just barely evident in the publication credits included with each essay. In the balance of this introductory note, I will take the opportunity to thank those who had a direct influence on this collection for their gifts.

A reader will soon note that a majority of the essays included in this collection were originally published in *Oklahoma Today*. I wish to extend my deepest thanks and respect to Steffie Corcoran, editor of *Oklahoma Today*. Oftentimes, a request from Steffie for an essay for a themed issue has been the sole impetus behind the writing. Not only does she request essays, she also edits them with a firm yet sensitive touch—she lets me keep my Okieisms while pointing out awkward constructions and less-than-my-best passages.

I am honored that she asked me to serve as a contributing editor for *Oklahoma Today*; I'm not sure that I've earned my place on the masthead, but I am sure proud to see it there.

World Literature Today also appears often in this collection's publication credits. My relationship with *WLT* began when I was a graduate student in English at the University of Oklahoma, where *WLT* is based. The Executive Director of *WLT,* R.C. Davis (who agreed to serve on my doctoral committee), brought me on board as a swamper: my roles ranged from hosting Neustadt Prize jurors to answering phones at the *WLT* office. My life was enriched by making the acquaintance of several *WLT* personnel: Programs & Development Czarina Terry Stubblefield taught me more than she could possibly know she did, mostly about ram-rodding big events and herding writers; Marla Johnson, Book Review Editor—the fruits of our professional relationship are evident in this collection's publication credits; Michelle Johnson, Managing Editor, whose wide-ranging interests and networking skills inspire me; Merleyn Ruth Bell, whom *WLT* had the good sense and foresight to hire as Art Director as she was completing her undergraduate internship with the magazine, allowed me to serve on the editorial board of the *WLT*-sponsored undergraduate literary and criticism journal —she also didn't mind when I dropped by her office to commiserate about my grad school experiences.

While the entire staff of *WLT* has helped me to grow into a professional editor, writer, and literary citizen, it is Editor-in-Chief Daniel Simon who remains a constant literary friend and mentor although I now live nine hours west of the *WLT* mothership. We got to know each other when he invited me to serve as a TA in his Literary Magazine Editing and

Publishing course. Daniel and I trade poems via email and request editorial comments of one another; he supplies both enthusiasm and first-class research assistance to my ongoing project on Oklahoma poets before 1930. Our most publicly visible collaboration began when he asked me to edit a special issue of *WLT* on world-wide working-class literatures. My dissertation was on contemporary American women poets of the working classes; Daniel's invitation and the ensuing months of research and correspondence with writers all over the world helped me broaden my literary horizons and sharpen my critical approaches. Researching, editing, compiling, and writing for the working-class issue ("Writing the Great Recession," November 2013) is the most satisfying scholarly work I've ever completed. I wouldn't have had the opportunity to put into practice theories about global literatures of class if not for Daniel and *World Literature Today*.

My literary collaborations with *Sugar Mule* editor Marc Weber began the penultimate semester of my graduate studies, in Spring 2009, when professor Catherine Hobbs introduced us after I gave a reading from my brand-new poetry collection on the OU campus. I sent Marc a poem or two, then he asked me to edit an anthology of contemporary Oklahoma writing. There was no such thing in existence, so Marc's request challenged me in ways I'd never been challenged before—although I'd recently started a small press, I'd never edited an anthology. Marc, as my folks would say, "turned me loose on it"—he gave me no rules, no page limits, no aesthetic requirements—he trusted me with it. The resulting collection was published as "Oklahoma Writing," *Sugar Mule* double-issue #35. Since most of the work had been done, I took the pdfs, added a few authors and works I'd missed the first time around, then published a print version entitled *Ain't Nobody That Can Sing Like Me: New Oklahoma Writing*. The online version is still up at *Sugar Mule*; you can read it—the poems, the stories, the essays, the memoirs—at *SugarMule.com*.

As if he hadn't suffered enough from my inability to refuse great writing due to concerns about a collection's length, in the summer of 2011, Marc asked if I would edit a special issue on "Women Writing Nature." I did, and once again, he didn't complain about the fact that I turned in a 160-contributor, 481-page PDF. I think of it as my literary-editorial *magnum opus*; I can't imagine an editor other than Marc who would have let it stand. During the months of editing, I made connections with 160 women writers from all over the US and several foreign countries—many of those connections have turned into supportive literary friendships, and I have Marc to thank for that.

"Women Writing Nature" also remains available as a PDF download from *SugarMule.com*. You'll see, as you read through this collection, that my relationship with *Sugar Mule* continues, primarily as a writer, although I seem to remember Marc asking me recently about editing another anthology. Demon for punishment, that guy.

There are many people who influenced this collection whose contributions are not hinted at by publication credits. First, I'd like to thank Lamar University Press editor Jerry Craven, who said "yes!" to this collection more than a year ago when it was as yet unfinished. We have spirited, often ornery, email conversations about writing and editing and strategies for staying sane as writers in red states. I don't know how many of you realize what a stretch it is for a Texas editor to publish an Oklahoma writer—Jerry's great sense of humor goes a long ways toward smoothing over the natural (?) animosity between denizens of two states separated by a muddy river.

The final essay also benefitted from an online conversation with a friend I knew from Wewoka, Richard Yahola, who is both a writer and an accomplished amateur local historian. Thank you, Richard—our discussion changed the entire course of the essay. Moreover, another electronic conversation with friends from Wewoka allowed me to write "Like a Fire in Dry Grass" without wondering if I'd alienate or otherwise harm many of my closest friends. You know who you are, Andrea, Janice, Myra, Angela, Sherry, big sis Pat, and Leon.

Finally, I want to thank all my Oklahomies. Oklahoma has several small yet vital writing and publishing communities—see the Introduction to "Oklahoma Writing" included in this collection. But Oklahomies aren't only writers who still live in the state: some have walked on, some have left the state for jobs or for love; some, like me, live elsewhere now, but spend extended sojourns back home where our ears can tank up on regional accents and our eyes can indulge in recognizing that particular cerulean sky, the quilt-batting thunderheads, the deep red dirt. Some are famous—nationally, internationally—many are not, but I appreciate and honor the folks who keep the local open mics going as much as I do the ones whose publications prove to outsiders that we're not just a bunch of crackers and hicks. We Oklahomies, we Oklahoma literary types, look out for each other, most of the time. We read each other, we review each other, we hang out together and share our work, we collaborate. We gather-up prodigals, those who didn't know we were looking for them—we claim them with pride, even if they don't know we do. This book would have never come into being without all ya'll, my Oklahomies. I'm beholden to you.

Jeanetta Calhoun Mish

The Arts

Who/What? Oklahomans/Writing

This "Oklahoma Writing" issue of *Sugar Mule* is patterned after the traditional question-pairs of journalistic writing: who/what, where/when, why/how. I chose to present it this way because in the minds of most people who do not live here, Oklahoma is an unexplored land, inhabited (if at all) by unexamined cultures and unknown people.

There is no doubt that stereotypical representations of Oklahomans abound: Indians in teepees; wealthy, obnoxious oilmen; poverty-stricken Okies; singing cowboys; outlaws like the Daltons and Pretty Boy Floyd. There are still Indians around—11% of our population claimed Native heritage on the 2000 Census—and teepees are still used for special occasions, but there are also Indian casinos and Indian businessmen and Indian orchestral-music composers and Indian writers and filmmakers. Not only do Indians live in Oklahoma, but also African-Americans (many of whom have ancestors who settled here long before white people did), Vietnamese-Americans, German-Americans, Irish-Americans, East Indians, Arab-Americans, Scots-Americans, Lebanese-Americans, and hundreds of other cultural and ethnic groups. "Okie" has been resurrected as a term for pride in one's heritage, especially among radical and leftist Oklahomans who work for a renaissance of the State's strong socialist past: Eugene V. Debs won 15% of the State's presidential vote in 1914 and 175 Socialists were elected to state offices that year. I'll refrain from commenting on the oilmen, since some of them are women and some are my friends and relations.

Cowboys and cowgirls still work the few remaining large cattle ranches, and many country music singers hail from Oklahoma. Outlaws now are not usually the Robin Hoods of yesteryear who, like Woody Guthrie's Pretty Boy Floyd, stole from the rich and gave to the poor, but are instead hard-core criminals who cook methamphetamine and small-time crooks who steal copper wiring, leaving entire regions without electricity. Oklahoma writer Jim Thompson documented the harsh violence of an earlier time in Oklahoma history, and that criminal culture is still active today. According to the Oklahoma Commission on the Status of Women, many of the people the state brands as outlaws are women: Oklahoma has the highest incarceration rate of women in the nation, many of whom are in prison as a result of defending themselves against domestic violence or because they commit crimes associated with poverty. Despite other negative indicators of the status of Oklahoma women, or perhaps because of them, there are more women contributors to this issue of *Sugar Mule* than there are men. Contributor Trixie Walther's raw and haunting poetry is based on her work with imprisoned women in Oklahoma. Recently, television has given us images of Oklahoma women in *Saving Grace*, and although the accents are never quite correct, the show does capture some of Oklahoma's culture, including its problems with alcoholism and abuse, the resilience of its people, and its romance with religion.

What's right about Oklahoma culture? Among other things, a genuine friendliness in most of its inhabitants, an active and growing green movement, and a rich, varied, and beautiful landscape, with its attendant flora and fauna, that is rarely recognized by outsiders. Like the people, the landscape has also been the victim of reductionist imagery: the Dustbowl, Route 66, oilfield boomtowns, Tornado Alley; the high plains. Although some of these representations are founded in fact, they do not fully represent the State. The Dustbowl was restricted to western Oklahoma, and Route 66 is only one of the state's literally thousands of paved roads (most mile-section lines are paved, or at least graveled; see Arn Henderson's "Base Line and Meridian" poem cycle), many of which carry economic refugees out of the state, or at least out of the small towns and rural areas, just as they did in the 1930s. The flat plains of the western part of the state leave most visitors completely unprepared for the steep hills, big rivers, and verdant crosstimbers of the eastern part of the State. The boggy southeast holds topographical kinship with Louisiana, and the wheatfields of north central Oklahoma merge with those of southern Kansas. While tornadoes are quite frequent in the spring and summer, some of the most common recurring images in Oklahoma writing are those of red dirt (*Okla-Humma*, Choctaw for red people/land) and of the constant wind. Another recurrent image is that of empty towns and abandoned homesteads: Oklahoma's boom and bust cycle has devastated many small towns. However, one Okie stereotype is true: we don't give up easy. (Yes, I know that is grammatically improper, but it's Okie proper.)

Oklahoma writers are not exceptions to this rule: we don't give up easy, either. It's difficult being a writer in Oklahoma, for many reasons. First of all, in many families, it's a suspect occupation—you're not really doing much but sitting there writing. From the outside, it looks like you're lazy.

Moreover, there exists in the state a longstanding dismissal of intellectual work. Secondly, it's extremely difficult to get writing with an Oklahoma flavor published in national magazines, a problem which holds true for most regional writing, except regional writing from New York or California. Third, there is a persistent problem with Oklahoma culture: in general, Oklahomans think that if something is from Oklahoma, it can't be any good, which is why out of state authors get teaching gigs at a certain state sponsored arts institute that, as stated policy, will not even consider hiring writers who live in Oklahoma, unless they got famous somewhere else. It's also the reason it's almost impossible to get stories about Oklahoma writers and publishers into major state and regional newspapers. Oklahoma does have a few well-known literary magazines such as *Nimrod* and *Cimarron Review* (published by the Oklahoma State University creative writing department which offers both an MA and a Ph.D.), but neither of them regularly publish vernacular writing. *Blood and Thunder*, the national literary magazine published by the University of Oklahoma College of Medicine, publishes writings that, as its subtitle states, are "Musings on the Art of Medicine," and therefore the journal does not actively search out vernacular work. The Red Earth Creative Writing MFA Program at Oklahoma City University published the first edition of *Red Earth Review* in July 2013; it does include some vernacular writing, in large part because most of the editors so far have been students from Oklahoma. I'll refer you here to Dorothy Alexander's poem "State of the Arts in a Red State" for another perspective on the difficulties of being a writer in Oklahoma. We don't let the obstructions keep us down, though. In good Okie fashion, since we can't seem to get our work heard or published nationally, we've decided to do it ourselves.

The good part of being an Oklahoma writer is that we have a grassroots literary movement that has grown steadily over the past thirty or so years. It can be traced back to at least the late 1960s and early-to-mid 1970s, to several poets, writers, groups, and presses, including the authors and artists associated with Frank Parman's Point Riders Press. There are currently a few small literary presses in Oklahoma includ-ing Village Books Press, Forty-six Star Press, Literati Press, and my own Mongrel Empire Press; these four presses recently founded the Oklahoma Small Press Association to help promote Oklahoma writers, publishers, and literary events. Several of the State's colleges have literary magazines, among them *Crosstimbers* at the University of Science and Arts of Oklahoma at Chickasha, *Arcadia,* an independent literary magazine established by former students from the University of Central Oklahoma, *Cooweescoowee* at Rogers State College in Claremore, and the *Oklahoma Review* at Cameron University.

Live poetry and sometimes prose readings abound in Oklahoma—in Oklahoma City: the Society of Urban Poets Open Mic at Ralph Ellison Public Library; a monthly open mic emceed by Dorothy Alexander, currently held at the Paramount on the first Sunday of the month; the final Sunday reading and open mic at Full Circle Bookstore; and The Vine Open Mic at Urban Roots in Deep Deuce, held every Tuesday night at 7p.m. Outside OKC, open mics, most with featured readers, can be found in Norman where Write Club hosts an open mic at Second Wind Coffee House and at the Norman Performing Arts Center on the second Sunday of the month.

The Gypsy Coffee House and Cyber Cafe in Tulsa hosts an all genres open mic—music, comedy, prose, poetry—every Tuesday night with sign-ups at 6:30 p.m. Shaun Perkins hosts poetry and storytelling events at her Rural Oklahoma Museum of Poetry in the small town of Locust Grove. One of the best open mics I've ever had the pleasure of attending is held on the third Thursday of the month at Benedict Street Marketplace in Shawnee; Jim Spurr is the heart and soul of this reading, where no one ever goes over their allotted time and where features can make up to $100 from the pass-the-hat.

Universities also host literary events in Oklahoma: at the University of Oklahoma, Oklahoma State University, and Cameron University, among others. Oklahoma City University, home to The Red Earth Creative Writing MFA program, and University of Central Oklahoma's Creative Writing MFA program, both host writers on a regular basis. Moreover, Oklahoma has an active slam scene, including Extreme Poetry sponsored by the Individual Artists of Oklahoma (IAO) and Red Dirt Poetry / Home for Wayward Poets which holds nationally-sanctioned slams and weekly performances at a locally-owned restaurant and sends a delegation to the National Poetry Slam each year; Oklahoma City native Lauren Zuniga is a three-time national slam finalist and a frequent TED speaker.

There is more: since 2005, a group known as the Woody Guthrie Poets reads as a part of the scheduled events at the Woody Guthrie Free Folk Festival in Okemah. Last, but not least, Scissortail Creative Writing Festival, spearheaded by Ken Hada (a contributor to this issue), is the homeplace of Oklahoma writing. Every April, writers from across

Oklahoma, and some who just like to visit every once in a while, gather in Ada (at East Central University) to read their work. Nationally-known writers read for fifteen minutes alongside beginning and mid-career writers who read for the same fifteen minutes. Hada's mantra is "Check your egos at the door," and the result is a homegrown celebration of creativity that easily rivals festivals I've attended in New York.

Writers' organizations are also popular in Oklahoma. The Oklahoma Writers Federation is extremely active, both its statewide organization and local chapters. Oklahoma Group of Experimental Writers was founded by contributor Grant Jenkins in Tulsa a couple of years ago, and innumerable creative writing and critique groups are found throughout the state. The Oklahoma Center for the Book, associated with the Oklahoma Department of Libraries, promotes Oklahoma writing, in part by awarding the Oklahoma Book Awards. There are no individual artists' grants available from state agencies, but the Oklahoma Humanities Council co-sponsors reading programs and Poetry Out Loud! in the public schools, and the Oklahoma Arts Council maintains an artists' roster which includes writers. All this goes to show that there's a lot of writing and reading going on in Oklahoma, much more than I think most folks would imagine. However, I'm sure I'll leave out someone's journal or reading series or organization or press here, and I apologize in advance; these examples are provided only to suggest the breadth of Oklahoma literary culture.

In order to have any hope at all of covering Oklahoma literary culture, I tried my best to get the *Sugar Mule* call for submissions out to all the corners of the state (there are 5;

check a map). The only rule I listed in the call was the writer had to be living in Oklahoma at the time of submission. This rule was instituted because most of the time when Oklahoma writers are listed (even on lists put out by state governmental agencies), the majority of the writers are long dead or have moved away. This is not to say that we have disowned Joy Harjo or Ron Padgett or B.H. Fairchild or Joyce Carol Thomas (to name a few of the living) or that we have forgotten Ralph Ellison or John Berryman or Lynn Riggs or Ai or Gogisgi Carroll Arnett (to name a few of those who have passed). Rilla Askew and LeAnne Howe, both of whom currently live part-time in their home state, and Linda Hogan, who has returned full time, were aware of the call for submissions, but chose not to contribute, because, I think, they graciously wanted to make room for new Oklahoma voices to be heard. This issue of *Sugar Mule* will introduce you to a small, yet, I hope, representative sample of the who—the writers—and the what—the writing—of Oklahoma.

"Oklahoma Writing" was envisioned as a topographical, cultural, and historical trip through Oklahoma. The poems are divided between two general headings, "When/Where" and "How/Why." The interpenetration of place and time is a marker of Oklahoma culture, one that can probably be traced to the influence of Native American philosophies; the category When/Where contains writings that explore the boundaries between place and time or that concentrate on one dimension or the other. "How/Why" contains writings that reveal the inner landscape of motives, of repercussions, of actions and their reverberations in the psyche. This is an entirely arbitrary division meant only to help the reader negotiate the terrain—roadsigns, if you will.

What kind of writing will you find here? The poetry varies, stylistically, from the vernacular, storytelling poetics known locally as "red dirt poetry" (see Jim Spurr's poems, for example) to cutting edge contemporary mash-ups and diastics such as those by Grant Jenkins and Hugh Tribbey. The personal lyric is well-represented, but often tinged with an unmistakable Okie accent; the poems of Yvonne Carpenter and Pamela Washington come to mind. Jonathan Stalling's visual poems based on aurally equivalent translations of Chinese phrasebooks are fascinating both to the eye and the ear. Slam poets Bryan Mitschell and Dezrea D'Alessandro capture their performance poetry on paper in the selections they've shared. Jason Poudrier's soldier-poetry, arising from active duty in Iraq and permeating his daily life on a farm in Oklahoma, is certainly among the best of its genre being written anywhere in America today.

Prose offerings include the quirky, sometimes uncomfortable fiction of Jim Drummond and JL Myers' unforgettable short story, "Wrestling the Wind." There is red dirt fiction, too, with Jeanne Dunbar-Green's "Since It's You and All" serving as a perfect example of the style. Detective fiction makes an appearance in an excerpt from Susan Miller's novel-in-progress, *The Kickapoo Cane Women*, while Susan Kates' creative nonfiction essay, "The Bird Watcher," combines nature writing and an exploration of women's relationships. In Danita Berg's prose poem/essay, "Head of the House," the author muses on her relationship to her dog and the sorrow of his (temporary) absence. There is more to read, both of prose and poetry, so I suggest you get started!

Where should you begin this journey through the nature theater of Oklahoma? You can start with Dorothy

Alexander's polemic "Civility in the Slow Lane" so you can learn how to go about being friendly in our neck of the woods, or you can choose to take a dip in Terry Ford's lake. You can skip down to the "W's" and join L. Michael West as he walks his dogs through Ada, OK or mosey on to the middle of the alphabet to be stunned by Laura Heller's powerful dramatic monologues or to indulge in Abigail Keegan's delicious imagery or to be shocked by Layton Isaacs's perhaps satirical poem, "Regional Delicacy." Like most journeys, it doesn't matter where you begin, only that you do!

Although I cannot name all the titles and authors here in this introduction, I want everyone to know that I am proud of every piece of writing in this issue and that I am honored to have made the acquaintance of the authors. I wish to thank Marc Weber for the opportunity to edit a special edition of "Oklahoma Writing" for *Sugar Mule: A Literary Magazine* (www.sugarmule.com); his offer was the impetus for this project of rewriting Oklahoma into the 21st century.

In a poem entitled "The Last Song" (1975), Joy Harjo declares, "oklahoma will be the last song / i'll ever sing." She knows, as we do, that Oklahoma is compelling in ways that can only be described creatively. And, like Woody Guthrie, each one of us believes "There ain't nobody that can sing like me." Therefore, I present to you Oklahomans singing Oklahoma. And, like Okies are prone to do, we are singing loudly, with pride in our work. We hope you enjoy your visit to the literary landscape of Oklahoma and that you find at least one image, one story, that surprises you.

In Memoriam: In 2014, Jim Spurr went to read in a slam against God and the Devil. We figure he'll win.

A Review of Woody Guthrie's *House of Earth*

It is customary when a reviewer has personal or business relationships with the author of a book she is reviewing to disclose those relationships. I consider myself one of Woody's Children: a leftist Okie poet who grew up working-class in a small town 26 miles from Okemah. Woody Guthrie's politics, his writing, and his cultural roots are reflected in my own. All possible conflicts aside, though, *House of Earth* is a richly-imagined, well-written novel that deserves a large readership.

Both of Guthrie's previously published books of prose, *Bound for Glory* and *Seeds of Man,* are usually described as "quasi-fictional," but *House of Earth*, while informed by his experiences in the Texas Panhandle, is Woody Guthrie's only fully-realized novel. *House of Earth* centers on Tike and Ella May Hamlin, a young couple who are eking out a marginal existence on a rented farm perched on the Texas Panhandle Caprock (not "West Texas" as the book's introduction states). Although they are living in the middle of a large landscape, the novel feels claustrophobic. The claustrophobia arises from not only the size of their eighteen-foot-square wooden shack, but also from their oppressions: by the weather, by poverty, by the rich farmer they rent from, by the nearly invisible yet palpable American class system. Mid-story, the Hamlins fall to a worse status than before because their landlord refuses to rent to them any longer and expects them to work on shares. Tike narrates this as his "Fall," from the ragged, precarious grace of being able to call a parcel of land *his* by virtue of a lease agreement to having "lost all of my hold on my whole world" and to "let myself fall so low, so damned low, as to end up being just another cropper!" (67). The dream that keeps Tike and Ella May from utter despair is to buy a piece of land where they could build an adobe house, a house of earth that would stand against termites and the wind, a solid foothold from which they could dig their way out of poverty.

Guthrie takes quite a chance, narratively speaking, in this story: for the majority of the novel only the two main characters are in view—only one other person makes an appearance, late in the book. Instead of populating the novel with humans, Guthrie brings alive the Caprock environment and its animal inhabitants as characters. The environment as character and antagonist inflects *House of Earth* with the tropes of both realism and naturalism: the Hamlins are heroic in the sense that they are fighting a battle not only against the natural environment but also against their socioeconomic status. *House of Earth* is a truly radical novel but, as opposed to some naturalist and radical novels of the early twentieth century, you should read *House of Earth* not just because it's ethically good for you, but because it is a novel of great skill, linguistic beauty, and emotional honesty.

Two New Working-Class
Poetry Collections

The year 2012 was a moment when working-class voices were once again heard—and sometimes heeded—around the world. And, if these two collections of poetry, *Smoke* by Jeanne Bryner and *The Pattern Maker's Daughter* by Sandee Gertz Umbach, are any indication, 2012 was also an exceptionally good year for working-class literature. Bryner and Gertz offer readers poetry which present working-class lives and peoples in richly-imagined details, evocative metaphor, and mastery of craft.

Smoke is Bryner's fifth book of poetry, and those who have followed her writing career will not be disappointed with this collection, but instead, along with those new to her work, they will find within it phrases, lines, entire poems that will linger in the heart and mind long after the book has been closed. Like Bryner's previous collections, *Smoke* centers on Bryner's vocation as a registered nurse, but it seems to me that in this collection there are more poems than in earlier collections on Bryner's childhood and her life outside the hospital. No matter the topic, though, the poems in this collection are crafted of finely woven, powerful metaphors that give me the shivers, among them recurring metaphors of the cleansing, healing power of water, of flowers which signal a radically empathetic perspective on beauty, and of birds, alternately figured as signs of emotional freedom or fragility.

The first poem of the collection, "Bed Bath," sets up a

33

collection-wide trope of the sacred within the human realm, proclaiming ". . . it is one of the holiest acts" to give a patient a bath in "the morning's sacred space" (9). Another ritualized bathing takes place in "Violets," written in the voice of a nurse attending to a ". . . girl with enormous / eyes and shoestring hair / who puts razor blades on her tongue, / . . . month after month" (55). The girl's life is "battered as a sparrow," yet, when the nurses wash her bloody body "the way you'd wash a mauled terrier," their ministrations initiate a turn toward redemption, a redemption brought about through a startling evocation of the beauty of flowers:

And when we close her skin
with suture, scars blossom pink scrolls
—rows of azaleas—like nothing
you can smell or taste, like little girls
in their eyelet sundresses
running toward you
their fists full of violets
crying, Here, here, love me.

Here, the poet references flowers twice, underscoring the empathetic shift of perspective required to re-value this hurting, battered child. Love is required to give to this girl a sense of her own beauty and worth, and, it seems, the ER nurses are the only font of love—a font of baptismal redemption created by the hands of human workers—in this girl's life.

The idea that redemption and healing are human practices as much as they are God's indulgences is revisited later in the collection, in "Where God Lives" (21), one of the poems arising from Bryner's childhood. The first two lines of the poem read "It is hard to believe in God, even now, / He was always somewhere else. Maybe fishing." God was some-where else when the speaker and her sister, ages six and eight, were left "alone with my baby brothers" while their father was out drinking. The speaker, the younger sister, went to take her brother off the potty seat and while doing so, "his weenie got caught in a crack / of blue plastic. Blood spurted as if I'd chopped / a hen's neck." Needless to say, the sisters were terrified and, without adult supervision, unsure of what to do. The elder sister "ran," while the younger wrapped her brother's wounded appendage in a wash cloth and prayed. From the speaker's perspective, her prayer was not answered by God, but by two neighbor women her sister had alerted, women who took care of the injured boy, gave the sisters "orange popsicles," and threw the obviously dangerous potty seat in the trash. On that day, the speaker asserts, God "lived on our street"—a pragmatic, hands-on god, much like the nurses and doctors and caregiving family members in Bryner's work.

Throughout the collection, it seems clear that one constructive response to trauma and tragedy is to contribute to others' spiritual and physical healing. Bryner's childhood of neglect and abuse and her efforts and wishes to help her siblings survive and overcome that abuse served to prepare her for nursing. In fact, it appears, as Janet Zandy has pointed out about laborers in general, that trauma and illness are prevalent among Bryner's hospital coworkers, and that each person's injuries and fears are both reawakened and partially exorcised in the practice of caregiving. In the poem "Kindness" (32), nurses trade out emotionally-difficult duties with each other: they make plans to cover for one of their coworkers who could not suction tracheotomies without vomiting and for another who whispers *"If there's a rape tonight, I don't think I can do it."*

The final poem of the collection, "Retired Nurse: Poetry Reading with My Patients" (92) reveals that practicing hard-won, creative responses to the ugliness of the world is a cyclical gift first given to the speaker from a woman who survived a concentration camp, a woman whose "violet eyes" are "a meadow of forgiveness." The gift is a survivor's imperative: *"Do something special with your life."* Smoke, as befits a working-class poet, is firmly on the side of a theology of acts: we are saved by the acts of others, therefore we should ourselves work toward forgiveness by engaging in redemptive acts on behalf of others.

In *Smoke,* God is a working-class neighbor, a nurse, a wife whose husband is dying of cancer, a doctor who saves a young, unmarried woman's life by telling her that her unborn child is not a sin. These angels of mercy are born from tragedy. And, in Jeanne Bryner's case, a poet was also born, a poet whose writing has matured into this collection, a masterwork of craft and emotional integrity.

Where Jeanne Bryner's *Smoke* is her fifth collection, *The Pattern Maker's Daughter* is Sandee Gertz Umbach's first, yet it already shows signs of facility with metaphor—extended metaphor, in particular—a good sense of line breaks, and a sensibility capable of working within received forms while making the form serve the content.

Similarly to Bryner's collection, Umbach's opens with a poem, "The Pattern Makers" (11-12) that previews most of the major themes in the collection while at the same time serving as an *ars poetica.* As the poet's father and the rest of Johnstown pattern makers knew,

Not everyone can be a pattern maker
old men on porches tell me.
You have to see things no one else sees.

In some ways, then, the poet is following in her father's footsteps, seeing things in the world others do not see and making (*poeisis*) of them the patterned language of poetry. The patterns in *The Pattern Maker's Daughter*, some of which are similar to those in *Smoke,* revolve around a set of themes and metaphors: an obsession with water—in Umbach's writing, water is not benign—illness, especially the poet's childhood seizure disorder, and the everyday rhythms and injuries of working-class life.

Anyone familiar with the history of Johnstown, PA will understand immediately why water would not be a benign presence in Umbach's collection, and for those who don't, Umbach supplies notes to the first two poems in the section that treats the 1977 Johnstown Flood. The Flood poems are of two types, one narrative and the other narrative-lyric hybrids that sometimes linger in the surreal, a combination that is very popular in today's poetics, but is not always as well executed as it is in *The Pattern Maker's Daughter*. As an example of the narrative-lyric poem in the collection, here is a selection from "Stationary Front":

the storm unable to escape the pull of valley air—
like all of us unable to lift up and fly over those ridges—
though thousands of us drove our Chevy's down Rt. 56
to D.C., Maryland, Virginia Beach, thinking we'd left it behind,
the shelter of green hills, the stories of our fathers' lucky strikes.
    The voices

> of those who stayed and those who came back, uncertain as the
>> lilting
> speech at the end of statements that sound more like
>> questions we could never
> quite answer—in silence when friends returned to the diner.

The first line of the first stanza reproduced here is the last line of a mostly narrative account of how the Flood began; at this line, and for the next several stanzas, the poem turns to a meditative consideration of the people of Johnstown and how the topography of the area has affected its human inhabitants and the town's propensity for inundation, both of the emotional and meteorological kind. Moreover, the next stanza's opening lines reveal one of this collections' most significant themes, and they also reference Umbach's most remarkable recurring metaphor:

> Folded into the crevice of those mountains, we are remote and
>> hidden,
> yet the storms keep finding us, our city's history a collective
>> memory . . .

Our city's history a collective memory. More than anything else, *The Pattern Maker's Daughter* is an unveiling of the patterns of collective memory, of History and of history, personal, family, community. To figure collective memory, History, and history, Umbach taps a formidable metaphor not utilized for this purpose, so far as I know, since Muriel Rukeyser's *The Book of the Dead*: she uses geological terms and concepts as recurrent, extended metaphors for working-class culture and history and poet-speaker's place within them. What might be surprising from an early-career poet is that Umbach wields her geological metaphors and references with great skill, in large part because she is obviously knowledgable (enough) about the geological structures and materials of Western Pennsylvania to use them.

Not only does Umbach put the geological metaphors to work, she is capable of creating the prophetic tone found in Rukeyser's *Book* and the great, communal "I am" of Whitman's work—both of which depend on concrete imagery as a launching point and which are difficult tones to pull off without sounding ridiculous. Witness this section from "Part of this Earth":

I am shale, common and conglomerate,
(the dirty inside of a purse, caked over lipstick
torn receipts and dried gum) skeletons
of organisms drifting. I am rapidly moving streams.
Carbon rich, organic, coal, compressed.

In addition to their use in the more philosophical poems in the collection, I found it delightful that Umbach's geological metaphors and language appear in unexpected places, and in doing so, solidify the metaphorical relationship between the working-class people of Johnstown and the geology around and beneath them—the analogy runs all the way through, like a vein of ore. It appears in "Milltown Girls in Flight," a poem recalling how the girl-children of Johnstown would hold their Barbies up in the air to make it appear they were walking "atop the crevice of Allegheny mountain gap"; it sings in the colloquial in a poem title, "Schist N'At." The geological ghost rises in two poems about the speaker's seizure disorder, one entitled "Headward Erosion" and the other "Fissile Flickerings"—the titles' geological terms are metaphors active through the entirety of both poems.

There are many more delights to be found in *The Pattern Maker's Daughter,* among them a series of work poems (using Jim Daniels' categories of "work" poems and "working-class" poems), several coming-of-age poems, and a scattering of poems in form: a sonnet, rhyming stanzas in iambic pentameter. The collection ends with the title poem which makes explicit the implicit connections between the father's and the daughter's "makings," bringing it full circle from "The Pattern Makers" at the beginning of the book. The poet makes her patterns by gathering "the random points I connect in poems that tie me to this earth." Sandee Gertz Umbach has created an extraordinary set of patterns in this collection, and we are fortunate that she has shared them, so we, too, can be tied to this earth and its people.

Both Bryner's *Smoke* and Umbach's *The Pattern Maker's Daughter* are must-haves for any serious reader of poetry, and particularly for those who are interested in working-class literature. Larry Smith's Bottom Dog Press has been publishing quality working-class writing for a long time, but, in my estimation at least, 2012 was a banner year for the Press, a year that saw the publication of these two fine collections of poetry.

Jeanetta Calhoun Mish

"Culture Warriors"
Reclaiming a Useful Term Appropriated and Abused by the Radical Right

My People

Are not quaint
They're not colorful
They ain't odd nor funny nor picturesque.
It makes me sore to hear or to see or to read
How you big long haired writers
Whack away at my people
Chew and cut and saw away at my people
Trying to make like you are their savior
Or their way shower
Or their finder,
Or their discoverer,
Like Balboa, like Columbo
Setting your maps and your charts and your pens
And stumbling onto my people
Like they was some sort of a new piece of land
Sticking up out of an old body of water.
　　　　　　　—Woody Guthrie

　　　I was going to start out here by saying that "ever since
Rachel Jackson and I started talking about her wonderful
idea for a progressive Oklahoma quarterly," I have been trying to get my mind around what, exactly, is Oklahoma's
culture. But then, I realized I've been doing that all my life,
partly because when you're from Oklahoma, no matter where
you go, you find yourself explaining that the Oklahoma seen
in movies (and now t.v.) isn't the real Oklahoma. I imagine

41

most anyone from anywhere could say the same. Nonetheless, since I consider myself a writer, and a writer's job necessarily entails representation, the question of how I represent the Oklahoma I know is an important one for me and has become an even more pressing question with the publication of the *Oklahoma Revelator*. How do I make sure that I'm telling my own bit of the truth from the grassroots, and not, like the "long haired writers" Woody Guthrie was chastising in the opening poem, either presenting "my people" as heretofore undiscovered exotics or presuming I can know and represent everything there is to know about them—about us!—measured and charted? As a writer, I must certainly be honest about our culture's shortcomings, but I believe I should also help uncover our strengths and reveal our potential. How should I go about being an Oklahoma culture warrior?

Over Labor Day Weekend, your intrepid editors and one of our contributing writers attended a conference in Albuquerque on "Building a People's Culture." Most of the folks there were veteran culture warriors, community organizers, and activists. And by veteran, I mean they were around for 1968; in fact, they were some of the people who made 1968 (as a cultural turning point) happen. We learned a lot from our elders, but we also learned a lot from a young woman under thirty who had been raised in an activist household and who continues to serve her own community as a culture warrior. We also learned humility while listening to a woman who had lived through—just barely—the bombing of Nagasaki, a woman who has spent her entire life testifying to the horrors of nuclear war in the abiding belief that she can help prevent another. All of us at the conference were struggling with questions of what constitutes a People's Culture: how can we build upon it for social good; how do we honor what's morally fine and sift out what's morally coarse? How can art, in all of its forms, examine, reflect, and represent the People's Culture? I'm not sure we ever came to a final answer, but we did all agree that while there are elements of previous decades' culture still extant and vital, that cultural events and objects are taking new forms in the information age.

I, personally, came to the conclusion that every time we evoke a culture hero from the past (Woody Guthrie, for instance) we should also look around to see who's doing today the kind of cultural work the hero did. I have gotten tired of hearing people say, "Oh, if only Woody were around." It's time for us to put our shoulders to the wheel. Woody's off to a well-deserved rest. But I do believe we can use models, so I'd like to introduce you to two people—Frank Parman and Woody Guthrie—as model culture warriors who have built their artistic contributions upon Oklahoma People's Culture. Alongside a recognition of our models' contributions, I'd like to introduce you to a few current Okie culture warriors, musicians and an artist. I'm not really going to spend any time on the first of my model culture warriors. Woody Guthrie is a spirit guide for the *Oklahoma Revelator* and his work is revered worldwide. If you're living in Oklahoma and don't know much about Woody, shame on you. It's well past time you surfed on over to the Woody Guthrie Foundation and Archives and got yourself an education. While we're speaking of musicians from east of I-35, though, let me introduce you to a contemporary example: the Red Dirt Rangers.

The core members of the Red Dirt Rangers are Brad Piccolo, guitar and vocals; John Cooper, mandolin, percussion; and vocals and Ben Han, lead guitar and vocals. Piccolo lives in Lone Chimney, Cooper in West Tulsa, and Han in Stillwater. Both Cooper and Piccolo are born and raised Okies; Han was born and raised in Borneo, but as Piccolo says, he is, like the other two members of the Rangers, "Okie through and through." They met at the legendary Farm in Stillwater, OK, where Red Dirt music was born. While "Red Dirt Music" is hard to define, listening to the Rangers' six albums will give you a pretty good idea of what it is: influenced by country, blues, and rock, particularly the The Tulsa Sound, and expressing a progressive politics and regional pride. In addition to their extensive touring schedule, Piccolo and Cooper host *The Red Dirt Radio Hour* on Oklahoma State University's KOSU, where they "play current and original Red Dirt artists, as well as artists who were influential in its creation" (available on iTunes). Recently, the Ranger's John Cooper taught an Oklahoma music history class at the Woody Guthrie center in Tulsa; the band has been involved with Okemah's Woody Guthrie Free Folk Festival since the beginning, and they regularly play benefit concerts of all sorts, giving back to their State and its people. Oftentimes, the amazing Randy Crouch plays with the Rangers; Crouch is often called "the world's greatest rock-n-roll fiddler." In addition to fiddle, Crouch plays electric, acoustic, and pedal steel guitars, dobro, piano and keyboard, banjo and mandolin; he is a respected songwriter whose songs have been covered by artists like Gary P. Nunn, the Zen Okies, Tom Skinner, the Burtschi Brothers, South 40, Vince Herman, and Jason Boland and the Stragglers. Randy Crouch has produced 21 albums since 1983, albums that combine rock and country in ways that no one but Crouch could imagine. But it's indubitably Oklahoma music.

For every so-called definitive characteristic of Oklahoma music, for instance, there is—what appears to those who think categorically—a counter characteristic: there is Bob Wills and there is the Flaming Lips. There is Lil Mike & Funny Bone and there is Michael Hedges. There is Hanson and there is the late, great D.C. Minner. There is Samantha Crain and John Fullbright and Idabel and Damn Quails and Applied Music Program and Leon Russell and Charlie Christian and more. While many of these musicians could be called culture warriors, the Red Dirt Rangers are culture warriors precisely because they make music from their own roots, topographical, artistic, familial, cultural, they don't kowtow to any preconceived notions of what an Oklahoma band should sound like, and they give back to Oklahoma and Oklahomans.

There is no doubt that there are misconceptions among outlanders of what Oklahoma music is—and not only among outlanders, unfortunately. If you don't believe me, go back and have a look at all those centennial celebrations; even the folks in charge of that series of events didn't seem to know what Oklahoma music consisted of, outside of the usual country music suspects.[2] Nor did they seem to know what it sounded like; as a case in point, I offer "Oklahoma Rising." I respect Jimmy Webb, but "Oklahoma Rising" is a soulless, unsingable, unmemorable, corporate piece of pap that sounds like it was written by committee for an Eighties advertising campaign. The same advertising campaign included many beautiful photographs to counter the astonishing but nonetheless actually existing perceptions of outlander folks who think the entire state is a Dust Bowl—still. There are others who think the entire state is a series of picturesque main streets, yet they neglect to mention the absence of people on those streets. Don't get me wrong; one reason I came back home after years of wandering in various deserts is because I missed the natural beauty of Oklahoma, especially those perfect early fall days, exemplified by the day I wrote this column: 76 degrees, clear blue sky; the grass and most of the leaves are still green and my tomatoes are as red as our first state flag. But, there are ghosts in our land and not just a few on the streets of small towns and Molly O'Connor's The Miss Oklahoma Project captures the haunted emptiness of rural Oklahoma.

The Miss Oklahoma Project, created with support from the Oklahoma Visual Arts Coalition, is a series of photographs of Barbara, "Babs," a lovely young mannequin dressed in motley finery and sporting a "Miss Oklahoma" banner across her surely out-of-proportion bosom. When the Project is entered through its main flash-based web portal, the photographs are accompanied by an otherworldly electronic soundscape designed by Jean-luc Cohen. The concept and photographs are those of O'Connor, one of the new guard at the Oklahoma Arts Council. She and Babs travel around the state, stopping at interesting locations; a few of the photographs are taken in cities, most in small towns and rural areas. Babs poses for her photographer in bars and flower gardens, on empty streets and in junkyards. The photographs themselves are lovely, lushly colorful, well-framed, lit mostly with late afternoon sunlight. But there is an undeniable strangeness about them; they remind me somehow of

Wallace Steven's poem, "The Anecdote of the Jar," wherein the poet places "a jar in Tennessee" that "made the slovenly wilderness" rise up to it. Like the jar, Babs takes "dominion everywhere," centering the Oklahoma landscape and built environment around her apparition. Although many of the photographs have been taken on recognizable main streets, there is no person other than Babs visible; her presence underscores the absence of vibrant smalltown life and challenges the observer to ponder that lack, its causes and its meanings. Oklahoma often thinks of itself as a mostly rural state, but can that autoperception be accurate when there is not one person other than this visiting simulacrum to be seen? This is not a trivial question; to ask it is to open up a series of questions about who we really are as Oklahomans and who we might become. Art is supposed to help us see the world around us in a different perspective, and O'Connor's The Miss Oklahoma Project does just that.

I'll return here in this last section to the second model Oklahoma culture warrior, who, like O'Connor, has worked both inside and outside the official cultural state apparati: Frank Parman. I've asked my friend and longtime Parman collaborator, Arn Henderson[3], to sketch out an over view of Frank's contributions to Oklahoma cultural arts. Arn writes:

Frank Parman has been one of the leading advocates of the arts in Oklahoma throughout the entirety of the second half of the twentieth century. As playwright and poet, he authored imaginative and original works in the voice of contemporary literature. And, as such, became a respected and primary stimulus of the avantgarde. As a co-founding partner of Cottonwood Arts Foundation, Parman's Point

Riders Press, was established for publication of poetry of the American West. Principal among those publications were volumes by prominent Native American poets Carter Revard, Lance Henson, Maurice Kenny, and Geary Hobson. Books by other poets included two volumes by the celebrated Wyoming poet Charles Levendosky, multiple volumes by Gar Bethel, and books by George Economou, Norma Wilson, Jim Linebarger, Mary McAnally, Michel Pons, David Slemmons, Ann Weisman, and the regional Point Riders Press *Great Plains Poetry Anthology*. The press has been cited as "among the best between the coasts." Frank also established a theater in downtown Norman for productions by emerging authors, served as a staunch supporter of the Contemporary Arts Foundation, and as instrumental in the development of the Independent Artists of Oklahoma, IAO. Moreover, he knows Oklahoma literature better than any other individual in the State. He has devoted years to scholarly research yet has seldom received acclaim for this activity. On a personal level Frank and I have been close friends since 1956 when we were in the beginning design studio in architecture at OU. Much of whatever I know of the world of modern literature I owe to Frank. I had to read whatever he was reading just to keep up with him.

What an education Arn has received, reading to keep up with Frank! Much of my knowledge about Oklahoma writing and writers was shared with me by Frank, not only through long and winding discussions full of historical and personal digressions, but also through his press. I own all (I think!) of the Point Riders books, and several of the Renegade series of chapbooks published as productions of the

Contemporary Arts Foundation.

One of the markers of Frank's artistic leadership is his multimedia, multidisciplinary, crosscultural approach to the arts—before that approach was widely popular, and before it was reduced to a set of buzzwords on grant applications. My favorite Renegade number is *Aggregate Images* (Renegade 21), which announces its multiplicitous approach not only in its title, but in the material production of the cover image entitled "Bale Out," (a title which itself holds at least a dual meaning). The image is a "collaboration of Gary Albright, George Oswalt, and Claude Anderson" a collaborative painting! Inside, on *Aggregate Images'* creatively-designed and laid-out pages, are more paintings, poems, reviews, essays on Oklahoma literary history, and photographs. You could put *Aggregate Images* up to any avant-garde journals of the period, from anywhere in the world, and it would hold its own, while at the same time showcasing home-grown artists. It is a travesty, as Arn mentions, that Frank has never received a lifetime achievement award from official Oklahoma arts and humanities organizations (such as the Governors Arts Awards, Oklahoma Center for the Book Awards, or the Oklahoma Humanities Awards). It is a tragedy that few people working in Oklahoma arts today know about Frank and his contributions or even that he is the single most knowledgeable source of information on Oklahoma literary history.

With this article, I hope to help remedy the tragedy; perhaps the travesty will soon be rectified as well. We can't take up the work of our predecessors if we don't know who they are. If I hadn't known Frank Parman, I would never have understood how much Oklahoma needs its small presses; his editorial artistry is sorely missed, and I hope that the small publishing house my husband and I have founded, Mongrel Empire Press, my coeditor's Red Flag Press, and our collaboration as the *Oklahoma Revelator,* can help continue the work of Point Riders Press and Cottonwood Arts Foundation. Frank Parman inspires me, but more importantly, he gives me shoulders on which to stand, a history upon which to build, and precedent from which to argue for the importance of Oklahoma culture. Thank you, Frank.

There is still plenty of work to be done by Oklahoma culture warriors; we here at the *Oklahoma Revelato*r want to help you discover who they are and what they're doing, and, perhaps, to encourage you to make your own contribution. We're just doing our small part to cultivate Oklahoma's radical roots.

Jeanetta Calhoun Mish

Meditative Presence
The Photographs of Craig Varjabedian

> I weighed everything by the measure of the silent presence of things, clarified in the racing clouds, clarified by the cry of hawks, solidified in the presence of rocks, spelled syllable by syllable by waters of manifold voice, and consolidated in the act of taking steps, each step a meditation steeped in reality.
> —Henry Bugbee, *The Inward Morning*

When we view the photographs of Craig Varjabedian, in this collection and in others, we often feel that something should be said, a response made, not to the photographer but to the photograph itself. A moment of embarrassment ensues as we admit to ourselves the irrationality of speaking to an image, the absurdity of making a considered response to an object incapable of speaking. But the chagrin soon fades, and still we stand before these monumental photographs searching for words: our initial urge to respond remains because the photograph has spoken to us. How can this be? What has it said? And how might we respond?

Over the years, several essayists have remarked on the capacity of Varjabedian's photographs to inspire a responsive viewing and a feeling of transcendence, but most comment solely on his landscapes or mention the portraits only in passing. I think this is because it is more comfortable to talk about transcendence than it is to discuss how the range of one person's art affects us. We are not culturally accustomed to speaking about our emotional response to art. We are culturally accustomed to transcendence: the idea that nature's glory engenders in us an experience of the presence of God is one deeply ingrained in our culture. But transcendence in art is rarely associated with images of people or animals or objects; it is most often evoked when discussing nature, and images of nature, such as Varjabedian's expansive New Mexico landscapes. Still, we struggle to express how Varjabedian's photographs call out to us and how they make us feel intimately familiar with and at the same time surprised and moved by the images before us. However, to label his images as transcendent is to ignore at least half his body of work, for along with landscapes, he creates astounding portraits and still lifes.

Moreover, because photographs are unique to the moment—both physical and emotional—when the shutter was released, I am not satisfied with thinking of Varjabedian's photography only as calling the viewer to experience a transcendent moment in which the image serves as a symbol of some divinity beyond. Not only that, but transcendence tends to revere silence—how can we talk back to divinity?—while these photographs clearly challenge us to respond. Nor does transcendence help us describe our emotional response to his portraits: for example, the portrait "Reyes Gallegos and His Newborn Goat," included in this collection. As we approach this book, which includes more portraits and still lifes than Varjabedian's previous collections, it is imperative to consider Varjabedian's works as a whole, to find a way to describe their hold on us that is equally applicable to the dramatic curves of light and shadow in his White Sands Studies and to the tenderness of the curve of Gallegos's fingers, which echo what can only be called a smile on the little goat. To describe the way that all of Varjabedian's works call out to us, I'd like to suggest that it is presence rather than transcendence that calls to us from his work—the presence of real things in the world and of our intimate relationships among them.

Before moving on to what the photographs say, we should first consider how a photograph is capable of speaking, given that it is a mute object. When we talk or read, meaning is revealed successively as the story unfolds. In contrast to the time-bound meaning of language, visual art speaks all at once; we intuit the "story" as a whole. What we see affects us emotionally, oftentimes without engaging our intellect. We have a "gut reaction" or our "heart is struck" by the images before us. The more masterful the artist, the more likely his or her vision moves us. The artist shows us a reality we had not recognized before and asks us to consider the relationships among objects portrayed and our relationships to them. We do not hear photographs in the same way we hear songs, but they sing nonetheless. Our eyes take in the sweeping curve of a cliff line, the shaft of light, the roiling clouds, and we clearly hear a greeting from the world. As Wesley Pulkka puts it in a 2009 review of the Ghost Ranch collection, a Varjabedian photograph "invites the viewer to fall into the landscape as if in a vivid dream." Indeed, it is to this invitation to enter into an intimate relationship with the subject of the photograph that we wish to respond.

But it is not only the natural world and its inhabitants that speak to us from Varjabedian's photographs. This is, after all, art, not unmediated reality. Charles Baudelaire, poet and art critic, declared that art "is the creation of an evocative

53

magic, containing at once the object and the subject, the world external to the artist and the artist himself." This statement is particularly true of Varjabedian's work, in part because he recognized early on the importance of paying attention and responding to the world's greeting. He waits, sometimes for hours, for the image to compose itself in the environment; he has learned the futility of impatience. Varjabedian himself has said that he looks "for images that feel like it felt when I stood there and that cloud moved over and the light did this." The resulting image, for the photographer, is as much an image of his relationship to the moment as it is of a mountain or a pumpjack or the person portrayed. Speaking of his work at Ghost Ranch, Varjabedian confesses, "I just somehow knew when I walked on the land at that place that there was something to do there. I was being called in some way." It is clear that the call to response in Varjabedian's photographs exists in part because the photographer is keenly aware of being called by his subject matter. The photographs, then, are crystallized dialogue, containing both the call of the subject and the artist's response; we have been invited to enter the conversation. The conversation includes not only elements of Varjabedian's response to the world but also his approach to the practice of photography.

When hearing Varjabedian describe his meditative, almost ascetic photographic practice and his sense of being called to the art, it is easy to understand photographic artist Andrew Beckham's assertion that the discipline of photography, in its rituals, its contemplative practice, and its "emergence into mystery and unknowing," is as much a form of spiritual discipline as it is an artistic discipline. In a manner reminiscent of Baudelaire's "evocative magic," Beckham's approach to the practice of photography underscores the idea that Varjabedian's photographs speak to us of both the world and of his own contemplative artistic practice. Through years of devoted discipline, Varjabedian has not only mastered the technical aspects of his art but also cultivated his aesthetic discernment, his sensitivity to moments of heightened awareness, and his perception of line, form, composition, and light. He has likewise become deeply at home in New Mexico, hiking for miles to discover an image, and becoming intimately acquainted with the land, its history, and its people during his sojourns. Varjabedian's photographs reveal to us intimate moments of meditative reality as experienced by the photographer in specific locales around the state. To say that his work has a "sense of place" does not quite capture the images' specificity; one might say instead that the photographs speak of the artist's experiences of the spirit of today's New Mexico, a place that is layered in history, inscribed with light, and sustained by its people.

For the artist to be able to share with us his sense of New Mexico, he must begin to understand for himself what it means; he must develop a philosophy of place. Varjabedian's philosophical practice closely resembles that of American nature philosopher Henry Bugbee. Both Bugbee and Varjabedian find their philosophy in the soles of their boots and in the moments of clarity they experience while trekking through the land. This land, New Mexico, has existed in partnership with its people for thousands of years, and Varjabedian acknowledges that the places he photographs are entwined in complex relationships with their inhabitants: "Ghost Ranch, and places like it, exist simply to exist. In so doing, they can inspire and instruct, they can transform and heal us and perhaps help us find our place and connection in the world." Henry Bugbee also understands the human element in the experience of nature as essential. In experiencing the world, we learn to be intimate with it, and that intimacy extends to our relationships with other human beings. When we become intimate with the natural world, we begin to feel at home, and we learn to see other people as an essential part of our world.

Not only does our intimacy with the natural world affect our relationships with other people, but human intimacy—the phenomenon of relationships between people—is deeply related to the way we choose to experience the natural world. The key is to think of ourselves as involved in coequal relationships with the world, not as ruling over the things of the world or as existing irrevocably separate from them. Just for a moment, try to bring to mind a person who is intimately connected with his or her environment—perhaps the woman down the block who knows the names of all the local wild plants and who tends an organic garden; she is likely also to be one of the people who regularly contributes to the community food bank. Or, perhaps, consider the way that the *mayordomo* of an *acequia* is intimate with and responsive to both his human community and the natural world. This is the sort of intimacy that Bugbee describes and that Varjabedian's photographs encourage.

Not only do Varjabedian's photographs and the wonder they engender help us become more intimate with the world, but they also encourage us to deepen our response to it. Intimacy requires that we are attentive to the person before us or to the natural world we're experiencing. We must be present, fully engaged, and paying attention in order to respond thoughtfully. In our contemplation of these photographs, we experience an intimacy with the subjects portrayed and with the artist as he strives to communicate to us the nature of his experiences. Photographer Jay Packer, describing Varjabedian's photographs, eloquently expresses this idea: "They speak of ancient, enduring relationships: those that bind humankind, the bounteous earth, the sustaining sky, and the light that illuminates them all." Varjabedian's artistic practice invites us to affirm our relationships with the world and its inhabitants as revealed to us in his photographs. It is this combination of the artist's meditation on the image in his viewfinder and his understanding of his presence in and relationship to the world that we hear calling to us from the photograph, demanding response. Bugbee understands this moment of meditative presence to be essential to the human spirit and to our experience of the world. Moreover, he believes that to have an emotionally rich life and to experience reality clearly, we must give "full heed" to what is before us—to pay close attention to the moment we are experiencing.

When we contemplate art, when we pay "full heed," we grasp not only the objects presented but also the relationships between those objects. Perhaps it is easier to explain what I mean by referring to abstract art. Abstract art, since it is nonrepresentational, is always about relationships: color and form, light and shadows. When we view representational art, we often place our emphasis on the apparent subject and forget that the artist has also composed the image to satisfy his or her aesthetic of relationships. When we look only at the thing represented, we sometimes miss the relationships represented. To return to the idea of transcendence versus the experience of meditative presence: if we view Varjabed-ian's photographs as symbols of transcendence, we are especially likely to miss the representation of relationships, since one relationship—that of the symbol to its transcendent meaning—takes precedence over all other relationships encoded in the photograph. This is not to say that a person should not see symbols of transcendence in Varjabedian's work; that would be as ridiculous as saying that everyone must. However, to give "full heed" to a Varjabedian photograph rather than asking it to serve as a symbol of transcendence is to begin to fully comprehend the extent of his artistry. The photographs allow us to join the photographer in his experience of things in the making, things as they are, things as they are received and felt by the artist. To give "full heed" to these photographs is to set aside our preconceptions and expectations, to refuse our mind's attempts to move on to other things and other meanings, to set aside our urge to view them as symbols of something else. Bugbee believes that this feeling of attentive intimacy associated with the appreciation of the world and of art can occur only "when we are ripe for it," when we have consciously prepared ourselves to be receptive. An artwork, a photograph, offers us all the same gift, but what we receive depends upon our experiences and emotional state. We must be receptive to receive.

What gift, then, does a Varjabedian photograph offer us? The gift of a meditation on our place in the world and on our relationships to it and to others. In New Mexico, the presence of nature, of landform and light, is pervasive, and Varjabedian's landscapes certainly convey the reality of that presence and our relationship to it. His photographic landscapes quite clearly say, "Linger here, and contemplate your place in this world." The portraits, imbued with Varjabedian's meditative photographic practice, also illuminate relationships in the world and the mystery of existence. Let us consider "Reyes Gallegos and His Newborn Goat" as an example of how our aesthetic experiences with Varjabedian's photographs speak to us of meditative presence and intimate relationships.

At first look, we see a man and a goat, foregrounded against a darker background of plant forms; the initial relationship is one of light and shadow, figure and ground. Next, we likely concentrate on the subjects in the foreground: Mr. Gallegos's face and then the goat. We see that Mr. Gallegos's straw hat and the goat's hair have similar tonal qualities, a creamy white as well as the soft brownish gray of the goat's spots and of the man's hatband. The man and the goat, in some indefinable way, seem to be related to each other, a feeling that is intensified in the manner in which Gallegos holds the tiny animal—a kid—cradled in his arms. Perhaps enjoying this game of resemblances, we go on to note that the curve of Gallegos's fingers echoes the curve of the goat's mouth, which in turn leads us to compare the man's smile and the goat's and the man's eyes and the goat's. But then we see that the lines described by the goat's legs parallel the stripes in Gallegos's shirt and we wonder if we have gone too far, so we step back to look again at the whole.

There we find another set of relationships: that of the man and the goat to the background, a mass of ivy, twining and chaotic, its darkness highlighted by a soft light that frosts the foremost leaves. Because the foreground subjects are set in the left third of the frame, the ivy commands almost two-thirds of the image, in a position of importance (we "read" left to right). The man and the goat are stillness against the implicit motion of the ivy; they are vertical lines and small finite curves against the unpredictable twists of the vine. The relationships between man, goat, and grapes is as important to the emotional impact of this photograph as are the individual components.

This photograph is not as simple as it might appear in a cursory glance: the natural order of things always carries with it a shadow. Relationships are rarely uncomplicated. Vance Gellert, photographer and curator for the Minnesota Center for Media Arts, reminds me that the relationships captured in images are not orchestrated by the photographer so much as intuited, that the magic of photographic art is that the resulting photograph reveals as much to the photographer as it does to its audience. It reveals to us our own world, seen anew, as if we were experiencing it for the first time. The portrait of Reyes Gallegos and his goat leaves us with a sense of wonder similar to that which radiates from Varjabedian's landscapes, and its call to respond is just as compelling. How much of this sense of wonder would be lost if a viewer's first and only response to this portrait was to recognize it as symbolic of the Good Shepherd? Again, this is not to say that this interpretation would be incorrect, but only that the intimate and complex relationships enacted in this image would suffer from such a reduction. It would take us away from the reality of this man and this goat and the world in which they live.

The still lifes included in this collection can also be approached and responded to in terms of meditative presence and intimate relationships. In fact, they seem to me to be less still lifes than collective portraits of New Mexican American culture at the end of the first decade of the twenty-first century. And because they are collective portraits of a culture, the relationships they represent extend far beyond the frame of the image. The photographer, the viewer, and the objects are so completely bound up in cultural relationships that it would be futile to attempt to name them all. But how else to describe what we feel when viewing "Buddy Holly's Microphone?" We are overwhelmed with a sudden recognition of widely shared relationships weaving like melodies through our lives, a moment that leaves us with the lingering feeling that the singer has just stepped outside for a smoke. Some younger people may not know who Buddy Holly is; nevertheless, I suspect that for most everyone, the image of the lonely microphone speaks of the loss of a singer and a shared song and, in that loss, of a diminution of all of us. Even the "World's Largest Pistachio," which in another photographer's viewfinder might appear ridiculous, is dignified and graceful, a study in light and shadow, curve and line. It has been saturated in the photographer's understanding of its genesis as a monument to a dead father and a remembrance of a communal pursuit. The relationship of object to photographer to viewer has been transformed by the artist's meditation on its meanings, and the resulting image calls for a response framed in admiration and respect.

Even so, it is not always necessary to name or to describe or to speak the response that we are filled with when contemplating Varjabedian's photographs. Sometimes it may be impossible. Bugbee believes that the only honest response to a powerful experience is a willingness to be transfixed in wonder, to be fully present, and that a deepening of our engagement with the world occurs as a result. This deepening of engagement is at the heart of the aesthetic feeling; it is one of the intrinsic values of art. One of the great gifts of photography is that it allows us to return again and again to a particular moment in a set of relationships, and to come to know the lines and shadows of an image as intimately as we know the backs of our hands. However, as Bugbee notes, "Nothing can be truly given to us except on the condition of active receptiveness on our part." He goes on to say that we cannot insist on seeing things "on our terms" if we wish to "fully comprehend them." To put it simply: we cannot accept the gift of presence offered by the photograph if we do not accept it on its own terms.

Therefore, I would like to suggest that we linger in wonder with Varjabedian's photographs and be immersed in them "as a mode of living in the present with complete absorption." One way to prepare ourselves for the intimacy of Varjabedian's photographs, for the reality of New Mexico that they portray, is to let the wonder of them wash over us, allowing the image to speak of the layers of meditative presence precipitated in the alchemy of silver and paper. We feel compelled to speak to Craig Varjabedian's photographs because they show us our world anew and challenge us to experience it deeply and intimately. In responding to his work, we come to a deeper understanding of the mystery of existence. What a gift we hold in our hands!

A Review of Linda Hogan's *Dark, Sweet*

From the beginning of her career, Linda Hogan's often prayer-like poems evoke liminality, speaking from blurred boundaries of animal and human, self and other, but it is the constant interpenetration of the sacred and mundane which poet-theorist Jennifer Gosetti-Ferencei calls "the ecstatic quotidian" that sets Hogan's work on a plane of its own.

Dark, Sweet includes poems from as early as 1978 and as current as 2014, and, throughout the collection, Hogan makes the everyday spiritualism of her poems available to a wide variety of readers by her use of spare, common language. Moreover, her poetry fuses the epic and the intimate in a Native American, feminist rewriting of Whitman's "merge" in which boundaries of all sorts are dissolved and the self / poetic speaker becomes intimate with all things, even with the birth of the planet: "In water / the world is breathing, / in the silt" (3).

Like many other Native American poets, Hogan's figurative language brings a decidedly political aspect to her work, as in "Going to Town" (11), where "The black walnut trees are gone, / stolen during the night / and transformed / into the handles of guns." Likewise, in "The Other Voices" (112), Hogan identifies the damage done by oppressive social practices, leaving us unable to speak our "inner truths" and equally unable to hear when others do:

Our other voices take sanctuary
while police with their shepherds

> stand guard
> at the borders of breath
> lest our stories escape
> this holy building
> of ourselves.

We don't tell our inner truth and no one believes it anyway.

An examination of human violence is a dark thread weaving through this collection. In the poem "Thanksgiving," we are confronted by the fact that human hungers are often only temporarily sated by violence, as she describes a "Turkey, blue head on the ground, body in a gleaming white tub with lion claw feet"(20). In the saga of tooth and claw, none of us are blameless, "All of us have stolen something / in the night" ("Coyote," 26) and "Even the trees with their rings have kept track of the crimes that live within and against us" ("The Light," 84).

Yet, despite human propensity toward violence and our alienation from the rest of creation, Hogan closes the collection with a section entitled "The Remedies." Among the collections many remedies are transformations in which "the story became a song" ("Transformations: Winter Count," 391) and another in which the speaker is like a firefly, "burning with life / until at last I am light" ("Wicking," 392), and the hope that we move toward and return to the light, that "...in the last breath / we give back all the swallowed / all the taken-in, and it is light, after all, / first and last, we live for, die for" ("Light," 205).

Linda Hogan's *Dark, Sweet* reveals the arc and breadth of a master poet's life's work. It is one of those pieces of light that we live for.

Looking for (Ralph) Ellison

I don't remember reading anything by Ralph Ellison when I was a Wewoka High School student in the mid-1970s. We read one Shakespeare play a year—*Julius Caesar, Romeo and Juliet, Hamlet*, and *Macbeth*. In my junior English class I remember reading Steinbeck's *Of Mice & Men* and Truman Capote's *In Cold Blood* (which caused a kerfuffle resulting in parents needing to sign permission slips; it also confirmed that our junior English teacher, Mr. Shivers, was not only cool, but was also serious about our literary education).

But no Ellison—not in class and not in the library, either, so far as I knew, even though *Invisible Man* was published in 1952, an essay collection, *Shadow and Ac*t, was published in 1964, and a few of his stories had been anthologized by the mid-1970s. I also don't remember anyone in my home town pointing out that one of America's most famous and accomplished novelists was an Oklahoman. Ellison returned to Oklahoma City in June of 1975 for the dedication of the Ralph Ellison Public Library. At a time I was between my freshman and sophomore year of high school, and I don't remember seeing any notices in the local paper or hearing about it on the television news, though it certainly had to have been reported. By the time I was a young adult, I had the definite feeling that I had *heard* of a book called *Invisible Man*, but I don't know for sure *how* I discovered that Ellison was a fellow Okie. I do know *when*—I was in my late-twenties, a period when I regularly spent time in the company of writers, many of them Oklahoma writers living elsewhere. During that period, I read *Invisible Man* for the first time.

The storyline of *Invisible Man* challenged me and angered me and and left a mark on my psyche that has never disappeared. Scenes still rise up, unbidden, in my mind's eye. The novel goaded me to see myself clearly, to hunt out and expunge any residual racism I was carrying around. I was equally astonished by the language of *Invisible Man*; to this day, whenever I reread it, I am again awestruck with Ellison's erudite yet familiar style. Take this sentence, for instance:

It was as though the uttered word had given meaning to the night, almost as though it had created it, brought it into being in the instant his breath vibrated small against the loud, riotous air.

I clearly remember thinking that if this Oklahoman could learn to write so magnificently, then maybe I could learn to be a better writer myself. Oh, not one who could reach the heights that Ellison reached, but a passable writer, one my family and friends, my fellow Oklahomans, could be proud of.

This year, when I returned to *Invisible Man*, I found the language just as moving and the story just as powerful as I had the first time I read it in the 1980s. I am sure that I understood more of the unnamed main character's trials during the three or four times I've read the novel in the last fifteen years—I've seen more of the world and have come to understand more about human nature than I did in my twenties. I had read only a few of Ellison's short stories until recently, when, in celebration of the 2013-14 Ellison Centennial, I purchased and read all of his writings in print. While

Ellison's greatest literary achievement is undoubtedly *Invisible Man,* it was while reading his short stories, collected essays, and his letters to writer and Tuskegee Institute fellow student, Albert Murray, that I met Ralph Ellison, Oklahoma writer.

It first dawned on me that I could find Ralph Ellison, Oklahoman, in his writings when I began reading *Flying Home and Other Stories.* The stories in *Flying Home* were collected and published in 1996 but the book contains stories written from 1937 and 1954. "Boy on a Train" and the selections known as Buster-and-Riley stories are particularly evocative of Oklahoma. Ellison's Buster-and-Riley stories follow their two little-boy protagonists around the neighborhood and into the woods, inviting the reader to experience the world from a child's perspective. Ellison based these stories on his own childhood, in Oklahoma City's Deep Deuce neighborhood, where he was born and raised. These stories are awash in Oklahoma atmosphere, Oklahoma landscape. I could feel summer's sweltery heat and see snake doctors humming by in the late afternoon sky. "Boy on a Train" is based on a train trip Ellison, his mother Ida, and younger brother, Herbert, took from Oklahoma City to McAlester; his mother had been promised a job there. Familiar landmarks and landscapes appear throughout the story: in one scene, after his mother teaches him the name for the tall, cylindrical structures he sees from the train window, James, the young narrator, muses *"Silo, silo. Almost as tall as the Colcord Building in Oklahoma City that Daddy helped to build . . . ."* In "Boy on a Train," Ellison not only evokes the sensory experience of Oklahoma, but he also, through the mother-character's voice, describes the almost-promised-land status the State held among African-Americans at the turn of the twentieth century: "We traveled far, looking for a better world, where things wouldn't be so hard like they were down South." Reading that hope today is painful, as painful as it must have been for Ellison to write it—Jim Crow came to Oklahoma, and the fluid social structures of a frontier state gave way to the Tulsa Race Riot and to the rigid race laws and practices of 1918 that saw Ellison, his mother, and his younger brother thrown out of the Oklahoma City public zoo at Wheeler Park because of their race.

Despite the sorrows and terrors of living as a person of color in early twentieth-century Oklahoma, throughout his life, Ellison referred, often fondly, to memories of Oklahoma, to its flora, fauna, and inhabitants and to the African-American culture and music that flourished in his neighborhood. The taproots of many of Ellison's essays are sunk deep into Oklahoma red dirt and Deep Deuce culture. During his lifetime, Ellison's essays on literature, race, democracy, American culture, and music—classical, jazz, blues, even flamenco—were published in influential magazines such as *Saturday Review, Partisan Review, The New Republic, High Fidelity, Esquire*, and *The Atlantic*. Some of Ellison's essays were previously collected in *Shadow and Act* and *Going to the Territory*; the *Collected Essays* was published in 1995. *Going to the Territory,* the title of which, borrowed from a Bessie Smith song, refers to Oklahoma—in Ellison's phrase, a "territory of hope" where African-Americans might find a safe and fair place to work, worship, and raise their children. Reading Ellison's *Collected Essays*, it's clear he never gave up on Oklahoma and its promise, seeing it as containing a seed of possibility from which to grow an American multi-racial, multi-cultural democracy.

Among the many treasures of the *Collected Essays,* three pieces stand out to me as essential Oklahoma reading: the interview, "That Same Pain, That Same Pleasure," and the essays "Going to the Territory" and "Hidden Name and Complex Fate: A Writer's Experience in the United States." In "Hidden Name," Ellison sifts through his memory to identify the moments in his life when the word—literature, writing— called out to him, beginning with his father naming him "Ralph Waldo Ellison," after the great American philosopher, essayist, and poet, Ralph Waldo Emerson. "Hidden Name" also contains a glorious passage that makes me homesick:

> So, long before I thought of writing, I was claimed by weather, . . . By spring floods and blizzards, catalpa worms and jack rabbits, honeysuckle and snapdragons (which smelled like old cigar butts), by sunflowers and hollyhocks, . . . By parades, public dances and jam sessions, Easter sunrise ceremonies and large funerals.

Catalpa worms! (Fishing bait.) Honeysuckle jam sessions. Ellison's evocative language strikes the tuning fork of my own Oklahoma memories—the reverberations last for hours.

The essay "Going to the Territory" combines an intellectual history of Deep Deuce's rich culture—and a remembrance of Ellison's early mentors—with a discussion of vernacular literature. All Oklahoma writers who make use of our distinctive ways of expression—Dorothy Alexander, Jim Spurr, Rilla Askew, Ron Wallace, the Letts family, and me, among others—owe Mr. Ellison a debt of gratitude for defending us, *a priori,* from those who would denigrate vernacular writing solely for what he calls "seeking the homeness of home": "there is no necessary contradiction between our vernacular style and the pursuit of excellence." He goes on to assert that embracing who we are is a democratic process, a "way of establishing and discovering our national identity" ("Going to the Territory"). Similarly, in "That Same Pain, That Same Pleasure" (originally published in *Shadow and Act*), Ellison discusses in an interview the fluid race relations of early Oklahoma and how they contributed to his development as an artist and as an intellectual: "On the level of race relations, my father had many white friends who came to the house when I was quite small, so that any feelings of distrust I was to develop toward whites later on were modified by those with whom I had warm relations. Oklahoma offered many opportunities for such friendships." Ellison was often criticized during his lifetime for his belief that a multiethnic American democracy, while still in the process of being created, was not only possible, but desirable and achievable. He formed that belief growing up in Deep Deuce.

It's clear that Ellison's Oklahoma upbringing is essential to his understanding of his profession as a writer and of broader American themes and issues such as democracy and race relations. It is much the same for me: for better or worse, I see the world through my rural Oklahoma upbringing. Like Ellison, living in The Territories allowed me stereotype-defying friendships and a rich vernacular language and culture influenced by Scots-Irish, African-American, and Native American traditions. It also gave me a hunger to know a larger world, glimpsed mostly through books discovered at school and in the library, and, for me, through Public Television, another Ellison-influenced project—he served on the Carnegie Commission for Educational Television. As an adult, I've taught programs and workshops sponsored by the Oklahoma Humanities Council and the Oklahoma Arts Council—both of which Ellison helped to bring into being through his work as a founding board member of the National Council on the Arts.

Ralph Ellison came home for extended periods several times, including a 1970 visit to lecture at University of Oklahoma and in 1986 to be honored by then-governor David Boren, who declared November 16 Ralph Ellison Day. Two of Ellison's letters to Albert Murray, collected in *Trading Twelves*, were written during Ellison's 1953 trip to Oklahoma. Ellison was delighted to be home and he wrote a rare poem on the topic, too long to reproduce here. But in his letter, Ellison's descriptive language about his home town also reaches the poetic:

> . . . boy but the barbecue is still fine and the air is still clean and you can drive along in a car and tell what who is having for dinner; and it's still a dancing town, and a good jazz town, and a drinking town; and the dancing still has grace. And it's still a town where the eyes have space in which to travel, and those freights still making up in the yard sound as good to me as ever they did when I lay on a pallet in the moon-drenched kitchen door and listened and dreamed of the time when I would leave and see the world.

This last year has been celebrated in Oklahoma as The Ralph Ellison Centennial—it lasts a year because there is some confusion about whether he was born in 1913 or 1914—and, Ellison's accomplishments certainly deserve at least a year of celebration, especially here in Oklahoma. Ralph Ellison never stopped looking back to Oklahoma, thinking about Oklahoma. He was known to quote often Heraclitus' axiom, "Geography is fate." In the Dedication to the original edition of *Going to the Territories,* Ellison wrote, "the territory is an ideal place—ever to be sought, ever to be missed, but always there." We as Oklahomans are still seeking that territory of hope, still learning to live together, to work together, to worship together, to raise our children together, to build a better Oklahoma. I, too, am seeking that ideal territory—a territory of the mind, of the heart, of the word—where I hope to meet regularly with Mr. Ellison, so I can continue to learn from him how to be an Oklahoma writer.

Oklahomeland

Western Civilization

The West defies easy definition. It's a paradox—a series of paradoxes. It's a place and a state of mind. It's a cardinal direction and a relative direction (toward the Pacific, toward the setting sun). It's made up of the Great Plains and the Mountain West and the Southwest. And maybe the Pacific West. It's a myth and a reality, a historical moment now passed and a historical moment still in progress. The West is often used synonymously with "the Frontier," but the frontier, like the West, has shifted, from the Ohio River Valley to somewhere farther west, perhaps west of the Mississippi. Or west of the Continental Divide. Or west of the St. Louis Gateway. Or west of the 100th Meridian. Maybe it begins in the Twin Territories of Oklahoma.

The West is a place that has been explored but remains unexplored. It's a place where land was said to be open and free. The West is where landscape is monumental—desolate and dangerous, beautiful and pristine, in danger of despoilment. It's the Great American Desert. It's where the skies are big and the landscape vast. Where the wind comes sweeping down the plains. Where the stars glimmer like diamonds on velvet and the full moon is bright enough to travel by.

The West, no matter where its frontier is delineated, has been for many people a place to start over or to make a stand and for others a place of banishment. Like the land we now call Oklahoma, the West has been said to be populated by no one, yet it's always been populated by Native men and women, and, later, by Spaniards and gringos. Oklahoma was settled again by tribal people whose families were removed to Indian Territory—at recent count, 38 or more tribal groups—and by African-Americans who came with them. By free blacks who built towns like Boley after the Civil War. And by Scots-Irish, Germans, Italians, Jews, Lebanese, and Syrians for whom Oklahoma held the promise of land good for cultivation or of jobs in the mines.

Frederick Jackson Turner, one of the most famous scholars who have thought about the West, made the following assertion: The West is a characteristically American place—more democratic, less authoritarian, less class conscious. Those who came to Oklahoma and their descendants believed that each generation would be better off than the previous one, especially in the seemingly classless state of Oklahoma, where people were more often judged by what they did rather than by who their parents were or what they had. Where oil made overnight millionaires and the harsh weather made overnight destitutes. And still the new Oklahomans come: in the last fifty years, our western state has been enriched by Laotian, Vietnamese, and Mexican immigrants, by just about every group you can name—even Texans.

Turner also said that the West is where the culture was imbued with "that coarseness and strength combined with acuteness and acquisitiveness; that practical inventive turn of mind, quick to find expedients; that masterful grasp of material things . . . that restless, nervous energy; that dominant individualism." The West has been and may still be a place to homestead, to build railroads, to think big. To take a chance, to light out to The Twin Territories of the mind, to join Franz Kafka's enticing "Nature Theater of Oklahoma"— even Kafka, a German writer who had never been to Oklahoma, imagined it as a place of reinvention. It may be true that the West is the incubator of rugged individualism, but it is also, at the same time, a place where people come together to build barns, harvest wheat, take care of their neighbors. Where, on April 19, 1995, America's gaze saw Oklahomans responding with selflessness, generosity, and resilience to one of the worst national tragedies since the Civil War.

The West has always had its travelers, those of the "restless, nervous energy," and they left their mark in the many trails and old roads of Oklahoma. Oklahoma is etched with the Trail of Tears, the Great Western Cattle Trail, the Butterfield Overland Mail Trail, Whiskey Road, The Chisholm Trail, the Cherokee Trail, the Osage Trail, the Abilene Trail, the Cimarron Route of the Santa Fe Trail, the Texas Road, The Great Spanish Road, the California Road, The Mother Road. Oklahoma has been investigated by Washington Irving and Thomas Nuttall and George Catlin and French traders and explorers, and maybe by Vikings. Oklahoma has sent out its own explorers like Capt. H.B. Hicks—his Comanche name was *Quanah Woshonga*—the "only man who ever accomplished the feat of circling the world—25,000 miles—on horseback" (*Historia,* OK Historical Society, Sept. 1909*)*. Like Woody Guthrie, who rambled all over the US and landed in Europe during WWII. And like Gordon Cooper, Owen K. Garriott, Thomas Stafford, Willian Pogue, and Shannon Lucid, all who traveled into space.

All in all, one might say that The West finds its most varied and elemental expression in Oklahoma. It's Indian

Country, horse country, cattle country, Strike-it-Rich Country. It's where the buffalo roam, where the deer and the antelope play. It's the wild wild West and the center of tribal worlds. It's a cultural crossroads.

It's where we live.

This Oklahoma We Call Home

The 8mm film is grainy now, with the passage of forty years, but, for me, the moment it captures never fades. A dark-headed girl in a cotton summer dress, maybe five years old, walks across a blooming pasture, side by side, hand in hand, with a tall, slim, black-haired man. They are laughing. That pasture was "the farm," the country place my grandparents owned. Grandpa worked in town at the Big Yank Blue Jeans factory, but he kept the land because he loved the things it demanded of him. My memories of my Grandpa are inextricably tied to the land, to his land, to this Oklahoma we called home.

I left Oklahoma when I was eighteen, to travel, to live in five other states and visit many others, to stay for extended periods in continental Europe, but I never felt at home in the landscape anywhere other than Oklahoma. I don't feel at home anywhere I don't know the names that belong to the land and its inhabitants, and I've never been as successful at teaching myself as my grandpa was at teaching me. Grandpa taught me the names of things that mattered—names of trees, flowers, plants, animals, fish. I'm sure some would say I didn't learn the "right" names; I call cicadas "locusts," because that's what Grandpa called them. But it's the colloquial names that matter, names that tell as much about the people who gave them as they do about the environment that received them. The bold yellow flowers with deep brown centers become black-eyed susans.

"This tree here, this one with the black bark, is a black-jack oak. There's a big oak, there by the lake, a granddaddy oak, white oak, they call it when they make things from it and down there in the gulley there's scrub oak and cottonwood and a red bud." "Meadowlark," he'd sing out, as a startled female puffed and danced and squawked to detract us from her nest in the grass. And when I protested that the Blue Jays were mean, always dive-bombing the barn cats, he'd remind me that it took a bit of bravery for a bird to nag a cat.

"Listen. It's a mockingbird. Your granny's favorite."

He often whistled back the varied lively birdsong, perfectly, and in tune, so well that he could maintain a private conversation with whichever bird he answered. Only the screech owls gave Grandpa pause. One spring, a pair of those white-faced birds decided to nest in the rafters of the little canary yellow house just twenty yards from his own, the house Grandpa had provided for his parents, my great-grandparents, to live in when they'd gotten to the age that they needed taking care of. I remember my grandpa turned pale, mumbled something under his breath, and took less time with the explanation than he ever had when I asked "What is it, Grandpa? What's wrong with the owls? There's a whole bunch in the barn."

"They don't belong here, nesting in a house. That's a bad sign."

And although Grandpa didn't like them nesting in the house—nor did his father—he didn't like the chore of moving their nest, either.

"Just shouldn't mess with owls."

My great-grandpa died a few weeks after the owls were removed from the rafters of his house and relocated to the barn. He just went to sleep one night and didn't wake up the next morning. Years later, I asked my grandpa if the owls were what my Seminole friends said, *stigini* or "ghost-owls." "Well, my people always said when they nested in a house, someone in it was going to die. And they did." Grandpa didn't speak his father's name for the same reason he didn't like the owls in the house rafters and for the same reason he threw spilled salt over his left shoulder and was adamant that the borrowed knife be returned to him in the same position it had been lent: open and butt-first. Some of those rituals came from the Old Country, some of them from Native America and they're all a part of my heritage. I find myself doing the same things and refuse to call it superstition—the popular phrase now is folk-legend, but my grandpa's "people," on his daddy's side anyway, were Delaware and Cherokee, and they just call it "medicine." From my grandpa's respect for medicine I learned to venerate mystery and to see sacredness in the natural world.

A sense of self-sufficiency is also part of feeling at home in an environment. Grandpa taught me that, too. If something needed fixing, he could fix it. And since I was always his "helper" I learned to fix things, too. I learned to handle a screwdriver and a hammer. I learned to put my tools up clean and in their proper places. I learned to catch crawdads with a twig, a piece of string, and some bacon scraps. He showed me that you don't have to go hungry if you know where to find possum grapes and sand plums and blackberries. Or black walnuts and native pecans. And that a fine meal could be purchased with a piece of fishing line, a long sturdy stick, and a hook, baited with the musty five-inch long earthworms that could be found down by the barn. Sometimes Grandpa would stoop down and cup a mint green grasshopper in his hand.

"Here, sis," he'd say, "this one is good for bait."

"Oh, yuk, Grandpa, he spit on me!"

"Aw, his tobacco won't hurt you."

I learned to change a tire. I learned that a sick cow can be slung up to the barn rafters with a come-a-long, until she's well enough to step out, then that way she doesn't get pneumonia. I learned to gather eggs and to pick persimmons from the tree in front of the chicken coop when they were deep-orange and wrinkly and sweet. Grandpa pointed out the difference between sumac and poison ivy, between copperheads and garter snakes. I attended calvings and learned how life was born; I watched the scours take most of my grandpa's calves in one year, and I learned that those that are born will die, even when you do your best to make them well.

I learned to see the world through Grandpa's eyes, and his deep blue eyes were always surprising, situated as they were under his thick black hair, and embedded in his walnut-brown face. I often gazed—and still do—at photos of my grandpa when he was in his twenties. He was movie star handsome, his lips almost feminine in their fullness, his narrow nose perfectly straight. He had a certain ease of carriage that belied his workingman's overalls and his cowboy farmer's dungarees. He sat a horse like a king. His hands were slim and his fingers long; they looked more like fingers that should have played the violin instead of the drums and the tuba he played in the Healdton High School band. I couldn't imagine those fingers picking cotton, but they had. I couldn't imagine those fingers shaking with poverty's hunger, but they had. I can feel those fingers now, rubbing the top of my head as I sat in the floor by his recliner, nodding off to sleep in the exquisite safety of his caress, to dream of walking beside him in the woods.

Grandpa had a particular, peculiar walk. He walked from his hips down, his upper body never moving, yet not rigid, either, but floating, somehow, above the mundane necessity of locomotion. His hips and his knees seemed to do all the work; his feet just tried to keep up. My granny said she could tell him a mile away by his walk alone. And he was a glorious dancer whose intricate, liquid footwork was hard to follow at first, but well worth the effort. His arms were long and his shoulders slim—today I wear one of his flannel shirts and it fits me well, although he was almost six feet tall. His feet were skinny, too, and the whole family knew of the quests to find shoes to fit Luther—they just didn't make them in his size much. Grandpa had a musical voice, a soft baritone that felt more like velvet than cotton. He was always whistling or singing or humming, oftentimes tunes he learned with his older sister and parents, when they sang together as a gospel quartet. He didn't talk much, though—the joke always was that the women in our family didn't leave much conversation for the men—and though the joke, like most jokes, contains an element of the truth, my grandpa didn't talk much because he always said that you shouldn't talk unless you have something to say. When Grandpa got mad, he said even less than usual, and a thin white line appeared around his mouth, the blood circulation constricted from the effort to contain himself. I didn't see that happen often, and I only remember seeing my grandpa cry out loud one time; when we went to the Hewitt cemetery, in Love County, to find his older sister's grave.

Juanita was the only older sibling he had, and had died in 1926 with scarlet fever. His folks were poor then, so poor she was taken to the cemetery on a flat bed truck where her own people dug her grave. They didn't have enough money for gravestone, so there we were in 1971 looking for Juanita's grave and the fifty-six year old man who had been an eleven-year-old boy the last time he'd stood on that windswept hill, stood sobbing because he could not remember exactly where his sister lay. I see him there still, standing beside a red cedar, struggling to regain his composure, the late evening sun pinning his long shadow across the graveyard. I never felt so powerless in my life; here was my grandpa, my life, crying, and I couldn't help him. I learned that silence is sometimes the only thing to say.

I've been gone from Oklahoma for a long time—most of 15 years. I needed to come home. The land calls me. I missed the trees, the abundant wildlife, the wind—and the smell. The sweetwater smell of cottonwood. The ozone generated by a lightning storm. Stink gourds and white primrose and Indian paintbrush and red and yellow honeysuckle. Wild onions and fresh-mown alfalfa. The part of Oklahoma I grew up in smells sweet, rich, smells funky, of humus, the rot of undergrowth, the bright succulence of new life rising up from the dead. I brought my son with me, my son who was born in a big city north of the Mason-Dixon line, and I hope I can teach him just a fraction of what I learned from my grandpa— I would call that a success. Grandpa died five years ago, and the last hours I spent with him, we sang together—a feat that astonished the nurses at the hospital, since my grandpa hadn't been able to talk for a long time; the Alzheimer's had robbed him of speech and self-sufficiency, but it hadn't robbed him of song. He didn't get to come home in the end; he's buried out in West Texas, a landscape he hated. Not enough trees, not enough water. We both did our penance out there; West Texas is purgatory for a couple of red-dirt-in-our-veins Okies, but now I've come home. And though his body still lies under the unforgiving West Texas sun, surrounded by barren caliche, I know my grandpa's spirit came home to Oklahoma with me and with his great-grandson, a young man with black hair who has a particular, peculiar way of walking.

Remembering Number Nine

I think it was alliteration that made Number Nine my favorite highway, the way it sounded like a chant, a charm. I was a poet even as a child, and would sit in the back seat of my grandparents' car, losing myself in the rhythm of the rocking road that sang its name: "number nine, number nine, number nine." I don't recall folks calling it Highway Nine in the Sixties and early Seventies—it was № Nine, for some reason in my mind it is always written with the old fashioned symbol for number, a capital "N" and a superscripted, underlined o.

It's not like Number Nine was the only highway around or even the most familiar one; my grandparents' farm was on Old 270 just a mile east of the intersection of Old 270 and New 270, at the New Lima Y. I knew both of those roads so well that I could close my eyes in the back seat of my mother's green 1960 Studebaker Lark station wagon or, much later, her red Ninety-Eight Olds, and know which turn, which curve, which bottom of the hill bump we'd just passed.

Nevertheless, Number Nine put a spell on me, and for most of my young life, and still yet today, I think of the topography of Oklahoma not in terms of "South of I-40" and "East of I-35, but instead, North or South of Number Nine. For me, "home" is south of Number Nine, all along its route. From Hobart in the west, where I was born while my father was working in Burns Flat, to Chickasha where my mother's family had lived before following the Big Yank Blue Jeans factory to Wewoka where I grew up, to Eufaula Lake whose muddy waters cooled us and fed us during cicada-hummed summers.

Some of my earliest memories involve Number Nine, specifically the Dairy Queen at Wetumka, where, when we were on our way to or back from Eufaula Lake, Grandpa could be counted on to buy Dilly Bars for everyone. We'd eat our ice cream in the parking lot, sitting on the tailgate of the truck. (I'm happy to say that the Wetumka Dairy Queen is still in business, and last summer, I honored the family tradition: while driving Number Nine in preparation for this article, I stopped there, and found relief from the 110 degree day with a Dilly Bar.)

As I got older, Number Nine became both the delimiter of my world and the tantalizing suggestion of something beyond. By the time I was 16, the highway had quit singing its name, and instead, as my friend Oklahoma poet Joey Brown writes of her hometown highway, 81 to Comanche, Number Nine began to call out "run, cut and run." And run we did, to Norman most often, at breakneck suicide speeds down Number Nine, sometimes bottoming out at the end of a hill, sometimes catching air at the crest of one. The trip to Norman was a pilgrimage: it was a mythic place, the bastion of learning, the cathedral of football, and the place to party. Number Nine to Norman gave us music—concerts at Lloyd Noble—and a taste of teenage freedom.

It would be poetic to say that when I left Oklahoma two weeks after high school graduation, I drove east or west on Number Nine, but I didn't. My mother drove me to the airport on I-40. I remember staring out the window of the plane, trying to trace Number Nine's route for what I was sure would be the last time. I stayed gone from Oklahoma for most of twenty years, but I dreamed of Number Nine, of hurtling down the highway on moonless nights, the headlights barely piercing the darkness, feeling more than seeing the animal movement at the edge of the road.

In 1995, I was living in Telluride, Colorado, and I needed to go to Vermont by way of West Texas where I would drop off my two year old son for a few weeks with his grandparents. I decided to take the southern route as far as I could, and talked a friend into making the trip with me, promising we'd sample the barbeque in every state. I had another, hidden motive—I wanted to drive the entirety of Number Nine, from the Texas border to the Arkansas border. I didn't want to admit, not even to myself, that I was homesick for Oklahoma. Instead, I justified the choice of route by telling myself that driving across the state might stop the recurring haunting dreams of Number Nine. We drove from Madge to Braden, stopping for barbeque at Van's Pig Stand in Norman. When I returned to Telluride, the dreams returned, more vivid than before.

The dreams didn't stop until 2003, when my son and I moved back home, not just to Oklahoma, but to Number Nine, to Norman, to attend the university. Later, I moved my mother and grandmother back home from North Texas and found them a place just a few blocks from the highway. It was in Norman that I met the love of my life, the man who would become my husband. I knew for sure he was The One the first time he took me to his house. It was on a ridge east of Norman, on Number Nine.

Broken Branches

The late winter sun had barely shown its pale face when my great-great-grandfather, JP Sanderson, awoke, rolled out of bed, and pulled his overalls on, adding a layer of warmth to the threadbare long johns and baggy wool socks he'd slept in. His wife had been up for an hour already and he could smell the coffee and biscuits. But he wouldn't eat this morning—it might make his bitter tonic less effective. Instead of taking his place at the kitchen table he'd built for Lou when they first married, he slipped out the back door and headed for the outhouse. It was cold—still below freezing—and the crunch of yellowed grass beneath his boots seemed louder than it had yesterday. Once inside the outhouse, JP pulled the door to and latched it, then reached into the small space on his right where the eave and wall came together. His fingers quickly found the small glass bottle he'd wrapped in newspaper and stashed there a week ago. Just as he slipped the bottle into his pocket, he heard Lou hollering for him from the back door.

"Guess I'd better go have some coffee," he said to himself, in the low, quiet voice he was known for.

JP sat in the kitchen for a good hour, tilting the hot coffee out of his cup and onto the saucer for sipping. Lou and him said nothing during the hour but that was not unusual; they were neither one much for talking even when they were young, and after making eleven babies and raising the eight who survived, there was even less need for talk. They knew each others' habits and assumed they knew each others' minds. A few minutes before 8 am, JP pushed his chair back from the table, nodded a thanks in Lou's direction, and said, "I'm going out to the shed. To see what needs fixin' before spring."

Lou nodded back and turned to the sink to wash the breakfast dishes in hot water heated on the wood cookstove. JP loved to go out to that shed and piddle around. Then again, there was no doubt one or the other of their tools needed fixing; on tenant farmers' wages, they couldn't afford to buy new ones.

Not five minutes after JP left, their oldest living son, James Harvey, knocked twice on the front door of house and came on in.

"Mornin', James—your daddy's out in the shed. Here, take a cup of coffee with you, to stay warm." James took the offered cup of coffee, thanked his mother, and slipped out the door. Later, Lou told the sheriff she washed and rinsed two tin plates in the time between when James closed the door behind him and when she heard him roar like a wounded bull. She couldn't bear to think their eldest was hurt bad—not after losing the three before him. Terrified, she pulled on her worn gray wool coat and rushed out the back door in the direction of the shed. There was James—still howling—and on the ground near where he squatted was JP, fallen half in and half out the doorway of the shed. In his hand, James held a small clear bottle. When she knelt down beside her son, she could see her husband was still alive, but she could also smell the sharp, sweet scent clinging to his overalls and she could see her husband's lips and tongue where the skin had turned white and begun to peel. Taking a deep breath, Lou gathered herself and ran to the neighbors' to ask them to call the doctor. When she returned, she found that James had carried his father to their bed where he died three hours later. The doctor was as sure as Lou of the cause of death—there could be no mistaking the odor and action of carbolic acid. On the death certificate dated December 29, 1913, Dr. Burnett wrote: "JP Sanderson, White, Farmer. Born October 15, 1855. Age 55 years, 2 months, 14 days. Drank carbolic acid and lived three hours. Signed: Dr. J. C. Burnett, Coppell, Texas."

The first time I heard that my grandpa's grandpa had killed himself must have been when I was thirty-six, in the year I finally checked myself into a mental hospital. The psychiatrist wanted me to write a family history of any mental illness that might be lurking, because he thought it might help him diagnose me properly and that it might help me not feel overwhelmingly responsible for all my less-than-sane actions.

There *is* something comforting about learning you're not the only nut in the family.

I had heard many stories about my granny's family, her mother's sisters in particular. Granny told her tales of crazy aunts with a particular relish, almost as if she took pride in having beaten back the family curse. When she told of the aunt who ran away manically hysterical at age fourteen and was found riding on the cow-catcher of a Santa Fe engine as it chugged down the tracks, Granny gripped the sides of her chair to illustrate how she imagined the runaway hung on to her precarious perch. When she spoke of her aunt the artist and shoe model who had "breakdowns," Granny walked over to where her aunt's expressive painting of lilacs in a brass pot hung on the wall and patted it as she patted my shoulder when I was in despair.

"My mother always said that her youngest sister, who drank hard and ran off with a bad man when she was 15, was not quite right, either," Granny added, meaning that of the five sisters, three were considered mentally ill. Granny's dramatics disappeared, though, for her last tale of family insanity as she related the trials of her own little sister who, for thirty or more years of her life, had been a regular patient at Big Spring State Hospital, diagnosed with manic-depression and treated with electroshock therapy. "Poor Polly," she sighed, and in the silence afterward, I filled in the family tree, broken branches and all. I thought I was finished with my assignment and started to leave the table, but then Granny spoke again, with something close to a triumphant tone, "Now wait a minute. It's not just *my* side of the family that has mental illness. Your grandpa's grandpa killed himself. And most of them, the men on both sides of his family, were depressed and drank like fish."

All my life, I'd been extremely close to my grandpa, a man I counted as my father. But I'd never heard him talk about anything like mental illness, and certainly not of his grandfather's suicide. Both my grandpa and his father, my great-grandfather who was twenty-eight when his father drank the poison, were tall, slim, reticent men who rarely spoke around company, who could hold a grudge for a lifetime, and who had both been known to have a temper when they were young. But crazy? My grandfather was the icon of stability for me, the opposite of the violent stepfather I lived with—it was hard to conceive of. I dutifully wrote down "suicide" and "depression?" next to the name of James Perry Sanderson. And didn't think of it again until a couple of years ago, when I found JP's photograph and a death certificate on a genealogical website. "Drank carbolic acid and lived three hours." It was then I realized that the great family secret was not that JP had killed himself, but why he did, why he did it so late in his life, and why he chose such a horrific way to go.

It's easiest to guess why carbolic acid was the method—surprisingly, carbolic acid was the most popular manner of suicide for several years in the late nineteenth and early twentieth century. Carbolic acid, also known as phenol, was used in Auschwitz, as an injection, to murder prisoners; it was the first antiseptic used by Lord Joseph Lister, but its use was discontinued because patients often died from absorbing the poisonous substance through their skin. Think Lysol (the two substances are related), with its uncomfortably sweet scent, but stronger. Similarly to Lysol, carbolic acid's primary use through the years has been as an antiseptic and germicide used for cleaning solid surfaces.

Deaths from carbolic acid became common stories in newspapers at the turn of the twentieth century. The headlines were often in caps: "TOOK CARBOLIC ACID: M. A. Cohn Committed Suicide at the Republican House Yesterday." "SUICIDE ENDS DRUNKEN SPREE: A Painter Kills Himself by Drinking Carbolic Acid in Wylie Avenue Rooming House." Alarming statistics showed carbolic acid suicides doubling year after year; one article from *The Pacific Pharmacist* estimates that up to 38% of all suicides at the turn of the century were effected by carbolic acid and that 85% of suicides by drugs or chemicals could be blamed on the substance. Doctors and pharmacists began to call for limiting the availability of carbolic acid, to make it more difficult to obtain for suicide and to slow the rate of accidental poisonings. By as early as 1904, some cities began limiting the sale of carbolic acid, which was usually easily purchased at a local pharmacy or at the farm store, where it was sold as antiseptic for barns and stables.

The popularity of carbolic acid could not have been based on the idea that it was a quick and easy solution. Carbolic acid suicide is a hard way to go. First, there is an "excitation" of the heart, quickly followed by twitches and convulsions. In 1907, Dr. Henry B. Carey noted that carbolic acid, while rapidly causing complete collapse and a shock-like syndrome, had a peculiar attribute: "the sensibility of pain is often preserved far into the state of collapse" (*The Pacific Pharmacist* 407). I wonder, knowing well myself the urge to suicide and its precipitating self-hate, if part of the lure of carbolic acid for suicides was its association with cleansing—perhaps one could believe it burned the soul clean on its way through the body. Perhaps killing oneself in such a caustic manner, acid burning through the esophagus with the pain undiminished by shock, served as a preliminary hell, one which a despairing person might hope would mitigate post-life punishment.

But all this still leaves me with the question of "Why?" In a 1904 *Joplin News-Herald* interview (in the state JP was born in and lived for many years), City Marshal John A. McManamy spoke of suicides in his city, among them many carbolic acid suicides. What drove people to commit suicide, according to the Marshal? McManamy declared, "Suicides usually follow debauches, or financial reverses. Debauches with the women and financial reverses with the men." But so far as I can tell, the Sandersons had been poor for a very long time—there seems to have been neither a financial reversal nor a worsening of personal financial status, although a 1913 article in the *Bonham News*, written by Peter Radford, president of the Ft. Worth Farmer's Union, decries the increasingly impoverished state of the farm laborer in Texas. Radford writes that tenant farmers' and farm laborers' "net earning power at best exceeds $150.00 per annum provided they are constantly employed." Maybe JP could no longer bear the heart-breaking, soul-killing, body-betraying poverty.

There were no great changes to JP's personal and family life, either, not any that could easily explain a suicide. JP was fifty-five years old; his two youngest two children, Katie Belle (14) and Mary Della (18) were living at home. The rest of his seven living children were gone from home, having started families of their own. He'd been married to Louisa for thirty-eight years. Several of his sons lived close: James Harvey gave the information for the death certificate and he lived in the same town; my great-grandpa Owen (Henry Owen) was living in Argyle, Texas, just up the road from Coppell, a town that, in 1914 "had two churches, two general stores, two blacksmiths, a bank, a hardware store, telephone service, a population of 450, and dealers in poultry, livestock, and lumber" (*Handbook of Texas Online*). Was JP ashamed that he had given his children no better life than the one he'd lived?

Were there national incidents in 1915 that could have been an impetus to JP's suicide? WWI was in full swing, but there is no evidence that either JP or his sons served, although they dutifully filled out their draft cards. The mostly guerrilla-style Border War flared in South Texas, but that was a long way from Coppell. On December 14, Jack Johnson became the first black heavyweight champion, but that doesn't seem sufficient cause, even for a Southerner. Maybe, I thought, it was the weather. Many folks who haven't spent a winter in North Texas may imagine that it's temperate, but that's rarely the case. It's cold and often wet in North Texas in December, and I wondered if a flood had taken the last of the topsoil from JP's rented acres or perhaps the deep winter had depressed him. But the weather in North Texas in December 1913 was not remarkable, except for the fact that about 3 1/2 inches of rain fell in one 24 hour period—a lot of rain but not out of the realm of the usual. There was no suicide note to explain his actions—according to the 1910 census, JP could neither read nor write. Not the weather. Not the war. Not the family. Not the finances. Still at a loss to understand why James Perry Sanderson drank carbolic acid, I have to fall back on my own experience.

On a summer day in 1980, I was driving my bailing-wire-and-duct-tape shit-brown 72 Ford Station Wagon south on highway 75. I had left Sapulpa, Oklahoma, that morning after spending the day and evening before with a friend from childhood at his family home. With a boy-now-man I had first had a crush on, then a desire for, then a longing for, since I had first run into him—literally—while we were both chasing a Coke ball—a foul ball—behind the bleachers of the Little League field at our hometown. My older brother and his were playing on the same team. From then on, he was the center of my imaginary universe, but I found out years later he never had a clue about my devotion. I imagined him going off to the hated rival town to date blondes whose fathers ran lucrative oilfield service companies; he told me he was usually out fishing or hunting on the weekends when he disappeared. I watched him act in the one play a year our school's speech and drama teacher coaxed out of mostly skeptical country kids and wished I could be his leading lady. We hung out with the same group of heads—partiers—so sometimes, if I were lucky, I'd sit next to him on the concrete picnic table bench at the lake pavilion, late into the night and far into the drink and drugs. I had gone to see him in Sapulpa hoping that he would somehow intuit my need for his attention. Without my having to say it, without my having to put anything on the line. We had twenty-four hours of friendly talk, but nothing more.

I had, the fall before the fateful trip to Sapulpa, washed out of the University of Houston in my first semester. The smartest kid in the small town I grew up in, I wasn't prepared for the university, and instead of rising to the challenge, I spent most of my time working in bars or drinking in bars. And now, I was living back home with my mother, taking a class or two at Seminole Junior College, and in general being useless. I don't even remember if I had a job—but surely I did, I had always had a job. Anyway, on that summer day, driving with the windows down (no air conditioner), 75 miles an hour on highway 75, I tried to take stock of my life, but the numbers wouldn't tote up. The flat spot in the almost-bare right front tire rattled the steering wheel each time it turned over and the thump it made sometimes jaggled the loose wire in the radio, randomly turning it off and on again. Heat-mirages shimmering on the road seemed somehow momentous and inconsequential at the same time. I told myself I was being absurd. Somewhere near Okmulgee a huge bug flew in the window and splattered on my forehead. I pulled over at a gas station, looked at my entrailed face in the rear view mirror and suddenly, the world shifted. I am not sure I can explain it any better than that. The world shifted and was riven; I fell into the crevasse. I don't remember the rest of the drive to my mother's home in Seminole, but I can feel it, still. It is rising up in me now as I write, a void in the center of my chest, an abyss. I keep swallowing, hoping I can wash it down. And maybe I'll be successful tonight, in keeping the darkness away, but on that day, the black hole located just below my solar plexus sucked everything near its event horizon into a swirling oblivion.

The rest of the story is sketchy in my memory, but I obviously made it home because that's where they found me, the ambulance crew, some hours later. I had taken all the pills I could find in the house and washed them down with a bottle of my mother's Old Grandad. Someone had called—I remember that now—but who was it? One of the guys I'd been dating, I think, had called, and, out of habit, I had picked up the phone. My mother later told me that he had been alarmed at my slurred, strange, jumbled speech. He called her at work (he knew where she worked?) and she sent an ambulance. I am grateful I don't remember the stomach-pumping. I woke up to a former schoolmate checking my pulse; she was working as an aid at the hospital. She was surprised to see me, thinking as so many others did that I had left my hometown to become a success somewhere else.

Like a Fire in Dry Grass

Through the bloody September twilight, aftermath of sixty-two rainless days, it had gone like a fire in dry grass, the rumor, the story, whatever it was. Something about Miss Minnie Cooper and a Negro.
—from "Dry September" by Wm. Faulkner

Another Negro Is Strung Up
Summary punishment for the killing of a Seminole county deputy sheriff was meted to John Cudjo, negro, about 30 years of age, when a mob of Wewoka and Holdenville citizens hanged the black to a telephone pole in front of the county courthouse in Wewoka.

After being drawn up, with a rope around his neck, more than 100 shots were fired into the body of the negro. The mob, believed to have contained more than 300 men all unmasked, then quietly dispersed and the town was quiet.
—*Cleveland County Enterprise*, 11/13/1913

My hometown, Wewoka, Oklahoma, seat of Seminole County, was founded by John Horse, a black Seminole, who, in 1849, established the first historical permanent settlement in the area. In 1913, another black Seminole, John Cudjo, was lynched in front of the courthouse by a mob with so little fear of legal repercussions, that no one wore masks. Despite Oklahoma's long and ignominious history of lynchings, I had never heard anything about a lynching in my hometown until one afternoon in 2013, as I was searching "Wewoka" in pre-1930s online newspaper archives; among the search results was a front-page headline from a neighboring town's newspaper that crowed "Another Negro Is Strung Up."

101

A year and a half later, I now know there were 153 documented lynchings in hometowns across the state. According to Charles N. Clark's *Lynchings in Oklahoma,* there were 111 lynchings in the Twin Territories from 1830 to 1907. Sixty-one of the lynchings took place in Indian Territory, 50 in Oklahoma Territory. Of the victims, 70 were white, 18 were black, 15 were Native American, 2 were "Mexican," and 6 were of unknown or unrecorded race. The majority of lynchings during the Twin Territory era were for murder, horse theft (lynchings mostly perpetrated by the Anti-Horse-Thief Association), and "unknown reasons." After statehood (1907), there were 42 lynchings: 35 black people, 7 white. Thirty-three lynchings were justified by murder accusations, 6 by rape and assault accusations, 1 as the result of a labor dispute, and 2 for violations of Sundowner Laws.

Editor Questioned
But on the other hand, we do not believe it is right to take a life before a fair trial at law, when a suspect is captured without. We realize that the white man is master of this world and in proportion as he metes out justice will his kingdom stand and in proportion as he minimizes justice will his kingdom perish.
—Editorial on the Cudjo lynching by M.W. Williams, *The Wewoka and Lima Courier,* newspaper of the all-black town of Lima, 12 miles west of Wewoka, 11/ 14/1913.

Statistics on Oklahoma lynchings reveal the shift from the victim-ratio of almost 4-1 white to black and 5-1 white to Native American before statehood to a ratio of 5 blacks to 1 white after statehood. When their plans to enshrine Jim Crow in Oklahoma's constitution was frustrated by fears that the constitution would be rejected by the federal government, state politicians passed a Jim Crow law on December 18,

1907, a mere month and two days after statehood was granted. Among the statutes in Senate Bill 1 is the definition of "negroes," as follows: "all persons of African descent are negroes, while all other persons are whites, thus, for legal purposes, limiting our population to two races, and including the native American or Indian population and all other races, except the negroes, as white persons" (qtd in Loudenbeck).

Those not from Oklahoma may find it puzzling that Indians were included as white in Senate Bill 1, but in doing so, legislators acknowledged four of the Five Civilized Tribes (Chickasaw, Creek, Cherokee, and Choctaw were slaveholders before the Civil War. Moreover, according to contemporaneous news articles shared at Doug Louden-beck's Oklahoma City History blog, the bill gained a large measure of its support among voters by reminding whites that, after the civil war, slaveholding Oklahoma-based Indians were forced by the federal government to grant their former slaves full citizenship and to share tribal lands and funds with former slaves remaining in their communities. Southern Indians' relationships to descendants of freedmen are still contentious for some tribes today, like the Cherokees, who, in a series of tribal decisions beginning in 1983, rescinded the tribal rights and enrollment of the descendants of Cherokee freedmen.

Additional fuel was added to the state's official Jim Crow stance by the popularity and (political) power of the Ku Klux Klan; historian Danney Goble asserts that, in the early 1920s, "150,000 Oklahomans loyally paid their membership dues" to the Klan (164). Given that only the 500,000 or so white adult male citizens were eligible for membership, as many as 3 in every 10 adult white males in Oklahoma were likely members of the Klan.

Woman Lynched by Side of Son
Mary Nelson, negress, and her son, 18 years old, were taken out of the county jail of Okfuskee county, at Okemah, Wednesday midnight, and hanged to the timbers of a bridge over the North Canadian river, six miles away.
—*The Shawnee News*, 11/ 26/1911

O, don't kill my baby and my son,
O , don't kill my baby and my son.
You can stretch my neck on that old river bridge,
But don't kill my baby and my son.
—Woody Guthrie, 1948

One of the most infamous, nationally-recognized Oklahoma lynchings occurred on May 25, 1911, the next county up from mine, in Woody Guthrie's hometown of Okemah. A woman, Laura Nelson and her son, J.D., were lynched off a bridge, left to dangle and spin from stiff new-rope nooses. Despite news reports, and, according the the US Census, JD was only 14, not 18. Laura had at least one other child, a two year old named Carrie, and other reports also mention a newborn. According to some eyewitness reports, Carrie survived but the baby was thrown into the river.

Woody Guthrie wrote a song about the Nelson lynching—it is rumored his own father was involved—and by the time Woody wrote the song in 1948, he had rid himself of any lingering Okie-style racism and the song remains a mournful protest, along with several other Guthrie songs condemning lynching.

In 2002, Terrence Hayes published "A Postcard from Okemah," a poem about the Nelson lynching and the postcard that memorialized it. You can see the postcard, if you're so inclined, at the *Without Sanctuary* website. I can't bear to reprint it here. Here are the last three stanzas of Hayes's poem:

> Now all of Okemah, Oklahoma, is hushed.
> Now even the children in attendance are dead.
> After that day in 1911, it did not rain again.
> To believe in God, this is the reckoning I claim.
>
> It is a Monday morning years too late.
> All the rocking chairs & shopping carts,
> all the mailboxes & choir pews are empty.
> I cannot hear the psalms of salvation
>
> or forgiveness, the gospel of Mercy.
> I cannot ask who is left more disfigured:
> the ones who are beaten or the ones who beat;
> the ones who are hung or the ones who hang.

Hayes's question, "who is left more disfigured," haunts me. I don't know if any of my kin participated in Oklahoma lynchings or watched them as if they were tent-dramas or traveling circuses. It is possible that they did. Certainly, my home state still displays its disfigured soul, electing politicians who write and pass bills to make it legal for businesses to refuse service to gay and lesbian people, to allow only people "of faith" to marry, and to refuse "that Obama's" healthcare plan and its Medicaid extension while at the same time cutting social services and refusing to require schools to install tornado shelters, and this after the May 2013 tornado when several children drowned while taking refuge from a storm in a school basement. This essay is a reckoning of the extent of my state's and my own disfigurement, the many ways in which race and race relations in America, in Oklahoma, and in my own life are still complex, difficult, and existentially important.

Seminole Burning

Spurred by the murder of a white woman by an Indian, a mob invaded the Seminole Nation and terrorized Seminole men and boys for more than a week before selecting two, who they took across the territorial boundary into Oklahoma to burn at the stake in a Baptist tabernacle a short distance southwest of Maud.

In the Twin Territories (pre-statehood), Native Americans were almost as likely as African Americans to become the victims of lynching. Tensions were high between white settlers and tribal people, particularly in the border towns, and particularly in the Seminole Nation (later Seminole County). Part of the tension resulted from the recently-passed Dawes Act which eliminated tribal ownership of land and, instead, divided tribal land into individual allotments, giving the "surplus" to whites. Whites resented Natives for holding land which they felt was underutilized; they considered Indians barbaric and lazy. Indians resented the whites living on land that was promised to them. Those tensions exploded on December 30, 1897, near the border of Seminole Nation, just east of the settlement of Maud, Oklahoma Territory, when an Indian man killed Mary Leard and harassed her children while her husband was gone to Oklahoma Territory (six miles away) to help his brother harvest corn. Although there was no evidence that the man who killed Mary Leard was a Seminole, the tribe was the closest in proximity to the crime. Therefore, a mob rode into the Seminole Nation to extract revenge, detaining, interrogating, and torturing Seminole men and boys, despite the fact that none of them answered to the description of the murderer given by Leard's children. After a week of unsuccessfully hunting for the man who killed Mary Leard, the mob, kept agitated by Leard's husband and other relatives, decided that it "would burn *someone*" to extract revenge for the crime (Littlefield 62).

Around three a.m. on Friday, January 7, 1897, with the approval of a crowd of 125 or more men, Lincoln McGeisey (age unknown; he is referred to in most accounts as "a boy" or "grown son") and Palmer Sampson, age 17, were burned alive.

The murder of the two innocent teenagers led to the "first successful prosecution of lynchers in the American Southwest" (Littlefield 170). Sixty-one people were arrested, nine received jail sentences, one received a prison sentence. The federal government paid $13,078.75 in restitution to 21 Seminoles for personal injuries, property loss, false arrest, and deprivation. Unfortunately, there would be no more successful lynching prosecutions in Oklahoma until 1922. The last documented lynching in Oklahoma took place in the town of Chickasha in 1930, 33 years after the Seminole burnings. Seventeen men were "charged with murder, inciting to riot, and destruction of property" for the last lynching in Oklahoma; however, "the case never made it to trial and the incident was shelved" (Clark 130).

As I write this section on the Seminole burnings, I remember that I went to school with, and played on the WHS basketball team with, Seminole students named McGeisey, Sampson, Harjo, Palmer, Tiger, Coker, Wolf—all family names listed as receiving compensation for injuries in connection with the lynching of McGeisey and Sampson. As is the case for many athletes, our Lady Tigers' locker room was the scene of interracial cooperation, perhaps the most intimate multi-racial space many of us will ever experience, where, in various states of undress, black, white, Indian, and mixed-blood girls sweated, swore, joked, teased, and discussed tv shows, music, make-up, and boys.

Lynching

In addition to lynching, racial violence had other manifestations. One was the "whipping party," in which a large group of whites whipped or beat a black person who was suspected of an offense of some kind. In 1922 alone, according to Oklahoma Gov. Jack Walton, 2,500 whippings took place.

Occurring in nearly a dozen Oklahoma communities around the turn of the century, a riot's usual purpose was to run the blacks out of town. Interracial violence occurred in Berwyn in 1895, Lawton in 1902, and Boynton in 1904. In Henryetta in 1907, whites burned the black residential district and established a 'sundowner' law, and in Dewey in 1917 a similar incident occurred. —*Encyclopedia of Oklahoma History and Culture*

Lynching is a term that covers a multitude of sins; there does not have to be a rope for there to be a lynching, since the term in its most general sense refers to extra-legal action against a person or groups of people. Hangings, home and barn burnings, "nightriding," whippings, tarring and feathering—all of these illegally-applied punishments can fall under the general heading of lynching. Then, there are "mass" lynchings, also often called "race riots." According to Clark's *Lynchings in Oklahoma*, in addition to the ones Everett mentions, mass lynchings also occurred in 1901 in Pierce, (Eufaula District of the Creek Nation, IT) and around the same time in Rosedale (McClain County, Chickasaw Nation, IT). Records of both these mass lynchings are scarce, and in the case of the Rosedale mass lynching, only one oral history of the event exists.

Unlike the Pierce and Rosedale mass lynchings, the

event usually called the Tulsa Race Riot is extremely well documented. On Tuesday May 31, 1921, whipped into a frenzy by an unsubstantiated report that a young black man, Dick Rowland, had assaulted a young white woman on the elevator he operated, whites invaded the Greenwood neighborhood, known at the time as "Black Wall Street," killing people and burning homes and businesses along the way. At one point, a machine gun was mounted on a flatbed rail car, hitched to an engine, and pulled slowly through the area, in order to more efficiently terrorize the community. It's estimated that, during the 16 hours of the assault on the people of Greenwood, 10,000 blacks were left homeless, 35 city blocks and 1,256 residences were destroyed by fire. The number of deaths has never been rectified: the official count of black people killed during the riot was 39; estimates of the actual death toll range from 55-300.

Earlier, in 1907, Henryetta, Oklahoma, managed to squeeze in both a lynching and a race riot in response to one incident. First, a black man named James Garden was lynched for the murder of liveryman Albert Bates, and soon therafter, according to an oral history collected from Anna McMahan, Bates's widow, the entire black population population of Henryetta was "encouraged" to leave town by roving white gangs led by the mayor, Dr. W.C. Sanderson, who "talked real loud to the negroes and ordered them out of town before sundown. Some of them left right then but others stayed a while. Several shacks were burned that night and they were made to understand the White (sic) people meant business" (McMahan).

As recently as the 1980s, a "Nigger Don't Let The Sun Set On You In This Town!" sign still stood on Old Highway 62 at the western city limits of Henryetta. I have seen it myself.

Prominent Citizen Killed
From all information at hand, it seems that a crowd of about
seven boys went to the hotel about 8:30 Monday evening for the
purpose of running the negro out of town.
—*Marlow Review*, December 20, 1923

From historical accounts, it appears that Albert W. Berch, a white man, and John Jernigan, a black man, were murdered for violation of a Sundowner Law, which, like Henryetta's post-riot ordinance, would not allow black folks in town past sundown. These laws allowed for exploitation of black labor, while at the same time prevented black people from living in the city limits. Lynching, whippings, and other punishments for violation of Sundowner Laws can be translated to contemporary terms as "walking while black after dark" inside the city limits which, in Marlow, OK, resulted in the shooting death of Berch and Jernigan. Mr. Berch was the proprietor of the Johnson Hotel in Marlow; Mr. Jernigan was his porter. A "gang" of seven young men entered the hotel "for the purpose of running the negro out of town" (*Marlow Review*). When Mr. Berch entered the hotel lobby, he was "shot through the heart and died instantly"; then, "his assailant turned and directed his fire upon the negro." According to the *Sandusky* (Ohio) *Star-Journal,* the gang was "attempting to force Berch to discharge the negro. Anonymous warning had been received by Jernigan ordering him to leave town."

Negro Assailant Lynched at the Scene of the Outrage
On Sunday the entire country north of the Rock Island was being searched, a large number of negroes from Wewoka and other points joining the drive. [. . .] (Henry) Conley's wife, with whom he fled from Seminole county last Saturday night, was located at Mill Creek, just north of Ravia, on Thursday. She is said to have declared that Conley had committed similar crimes before and made her help him to get away.
—*The Shawnee Daily News-Herald*, 11/17/1917

I was half-way through the final draft of this essay when a friend from my hometown, another writer and an accomplished amateur local historian, contacted me to say that he'd heard from a couple of old men that there was another lynching in our town in 1917, four years after the Cudjo lynching. After checking *Lynching in Oklahoma,* I found a 1917 lynching listed as occurring in Holdenville, six miles away. Returning to the newspaper archive, I searched for "Henry Conley," the man who was named as lynched in Holdenville for the rape of Mrs. Jessee Burford, a Wewoka resident.

According to contemporaneous newspaper accounts, while Conley had been returned to Holdenville on the train after being captured in another county, the posse that spirited him away from the depot was composed of Wewokans, and he was hanged in Wewoka, at the home of the woman he was accused of raping. According to one man who was a child at the time and who witnessed the proceedings, Conley was "paraded" in an open wagon up Highway 56 from Holdenville to Wewoka then north of town six miles to the Burford's farm where the posse hung him from a tree and fired shots into his body. One of the elderly gentlemen who confessed to this second Wewoka lynching was a young judge in 1917. He told my friend that someone came to his house and asked him if he wanted to stop the lynching. He said he would deal with it later; when he got around to doing something, the lynching had already occurred.

On his deathbed, the old judge said his lack of action was his greatest regret.

OU President David Boren Expels Two Students for Involvement in Racist Video

University of Oklahoma President David Boren has expelled two students identified as leaders in a racist chant video recorded at an SAE fraternity event.
—*KOCO.com*, 3/10/2015

In the years between Oklahoma's last documented lynching in 1930 and my birth in 1961, the Civil Rights Movement fomented changes in Oklahoma as it did in the rest of the country. In 1946, willing to endure years of delay to her career in order to bring Oklahoma's discriminatory practices to the courts, Ada Lois Sipuel (Fisher) applied to law school at the University of Oklahoma. She was denied because of race. In 1948, the US Supreme Court ruled that the state of Oklahoma must provide instruction for blacks equal to that of whites. In response, the state created a law school at historically-black Langston University, but further litigation proved that the hastily-instituted law school was "inferior" to the OU School of law and therefore not an equal educational opportunity. OU was forced to admit Sipuel in 1949; she sat in a chair marked "colored" that was blocked off by a chain from the white students. George McLauren, a black man seeking admission to OU's graduate school in 1948, faced a similar struggle; initially denied admittance because of his race, after a court case, he gained admittance although, like Sipuel, he was required to study in a separated area within the law library and to eat lunch in segregation.

Such courage they showed, Sipuel and McLauren, matriculating at OU, where, just 24 years earlier, Edwin C. DeBarr, one of the four founding faculty members, first head of the Department of Chemistry, and, later, Vice-President of the University, also served as the Grand Dragon of the Oklahoma Realm of the Imperial Knights of the Ku Klux Klan.

Oklahoma City African Americans Sit-in for Integration, 1958-64

They sat quietly at the lunch counter and ordered their Cokes. When they were refused service, they continued to sit in silence as the surrounding white customers unleashed a wave of threats and racial slurs. The manager called the police, who arrived and hovered over the children as the crowd of hecklers grew in size.
—*Global Nonviolent Action Database*

In August 1958, Clara Luper, an African-American public school teacher director of the local NAACP Youth Council, took 13 children, ages 6-13, to the segregated lunch counter of Katz's Drug in downtown Oklahoma City. It took two days of sitting at the counter in shifts, two days of harassment, two days of courage and fear, before an employee served one of the children a hamburger. In 1968, Hannah Diggs Atkins was elected Oklahoma's first female African American legislator. In 1952, Oklahoma City native Ralph Ellison, who grew up not too far from Katz's Drug, published *Invisible Man*.

My hometown schools began the integration process by integrating the sports teams first, beginning in the fall of

1957 when my youngest uncle was a sophomore. According to my uncle, "We, as athletes, had absolutely no difficulty blending. The blacks attended Douglas High and we went to Wewoka High. Complete integration was accomplished by 1964. Your aunt indicates that in junior high some limited black vs. white problems arose, primarily with the girls challenging one another."

Yet, despite all this "progress" dearly purchased with the blood, sweat, and tears of people of color, when *Oklahoma Today* published its first African-American issue in January of 2015, the editors received hate mail.

The Lynching at Wewoka

It is true that the white people of this town and neighborhood hanged and fired about 100 shots with pistols and all sorts of guns into John Cudjo's body, on the night of the 4th inst., on a telephone pole in front of the courthouse. We had no trouble hearing the guns and screams of white women, a few of whom found they could not stand the ordeal. The wife of the under sheriff, whom John Cudjo had killed the previous Saturday night, asked that Cudjo be not burned; so the barrel of oil and roll of cotton bagging carried over to roll him in were not used, but returned to their owners.

—*The Crisis* #7, Journal of the NAACP, January 1914

When I was growing up in Wewoka between 1962 and 1979, the population was 5500; by race, it was about 50% white, 20% Black, and 20% Native American—the last 10%, "Other." The demographic of my friends was more like 35% white, 35% black, and 20% Native American—partly because I was a Head Start kid and partly because I was often uncomfortable and sometimes unwelcome around the white, middle-class students whose parents belonged to the Country Club.

Although Wewoka was a small town, we had a black community center and a white community center, a black swimming pool and a white swimming pool; a black library and a white library. In all things except school, we were segregated, even at death: there were black cemeteries and white cemeteries and Indian cemeteries. Where did the Indian kids fit in this black/white schema? Well, it depended. Some Creeks and Seminoles, since they'd been intermarrying with African-Americans for years, hung out with the black kids. Others hung out with the white kids, especially those whose parents were middle class and those who played football or were in the band or in Campfire Girls. Mostly, though, the Indian kids stayed to themselves, particularly those who came from traditional families.

Or, at least, that's the way it seemed to me. Recently, I've come to realize that I knew very little about most of my classmates' lives, other than the handful of people I counted as my intimates. I knew that my best girl friend, the one who'd saved me on my first day of kindergarten when I got lost walking down to the Head Start after morning classes—the one who, in 1977, came out as a lesbian in our small rural town—was living on her own during high school, in the trailer she'd once shared with her mother and half-brother. I knew that a boy I liked was also living alone, escaping an abusive and alcoholic father, supporting himself by working in the oilfields on morning tower, from 10pm to 6am; after work, he showered, changed clothes and went to school. I was invited into only one black classmate's home the entire time I lived there, and, so long as I was living in my stepfathers' house, I invited no black classmates. There was an unspoken understanding that although our generation might be evolving toward more progressive race relations, our parents and grandparents, both black and white, were not.

In high school, I hung out mostly with "the heads": the partiers, the drinkers, the potheads. I also spent some time "over to nigger town" as most of my family would say. I called it the place where my friends had the best after-basketball-and-football-game dances. After games, the white middle-class kids all went to some other white middle class kid's house to drink and screw. I was not invited and probably wouldn't have gone if I were. Home basketball and football games were Friday, and for a while, every Friday night took me over to the black community center to *dance the night away*. I loved to dance, and I needed lessons, too, or at least that's what A.B. said the first time I danced with my black friends.

"All you white girls," she said, arms crossed, shaking her head, "ain't none-uh you knows how to shake your booty."

A.B. and J. and T. and M. and S. and A.E. taught me a complex version of the Bump and coached me in the Bus Stop and its love child, the Hustle, which was enormously popular after *Saturday Night Fever* came out in December 1977, halfway through my junior year. I was lovingly tutored in the black-girl groove: upper body mostly still, drop the hips with knees bent slightly, swing hips side to side in time to the music, while the feet moved in a circle, or shifted left and right or forward and back. The hips did the work. It wasn't twerking; it was graceful and classy and sexy, and worked with most any song; it also got me through the jiving and hollering of a show-off Stroll.

A Night of Vengeance in Wewoka

Mrs. Dennis, wife of the murdered deputy, had been brought downtown to observe the public spectacle. Across the street

from the courthouse she and her seven (now fatherless) children sat in the front office of the Wewoka Democrat newspaper and watched as her husband's killer [Cudjo] was lynched and shot to pieces.
  —Butler 185

Most importantly, for my teenaged awkward self, the dances I learned didn't have any of those idiotic moves the rest of the white kids were trying out on their dates, no funky chicken, no disco duck. While the girls were grooving, the black boys got down, inventing proto-break-dancing by combining a modern version of the buck and the straight jig with The Worm and funk-inspired popping and locking. We were all influenced by Michael Jackson, P-Funk, Kool & the Gang, and Sly, icons whose sounds we gorged ourselves on whenever we had a chance in those pre-MTV, pre-BET years, on *The Jackson Five* and later, *The Jacksons,* and *Soul Train* and *The Midnight Special* tv shows. Shows I wasn't allowed to watch until after my mother divorced my stepfather, the stepfather who thought *All in the Family* was a paean to his white-race-superiority philosophy. No "goddamn nigger shows" in his house.

Negro Lynched
[. . .] The officers were overpowered, after which the negro was turned over to a party of men and boys who hurried him cross-country to the home of the woman [Mrs. Burford] he was charged with attacking while she was alone in a cornfield. En route the crowd was augumented (sic.) by several hundred men, women, and children residents of Seminole and Hughes counties. [. . .] As Conley was swung into the air the victim of his lust shot six bullets from an automobile into his body.
—*Norman Daily Transcript,* 6/18/1917

There are two documented lynchings of women in Oklahoma: one, Mary Nelson, the other, Marie Scott (Wagoner County, 1914). It will take another essay to suss out the complexities of women's roles in Oklahoma lynchings, as accusers, as victims, as executioners' right hand, as avenging "angels," as wives, and as partners and family members suffering collateral damage, sustaining the loss of their husbands and sons and brothers and fathers and often their homes and livelihoods.

One night at 3am, after I returned from dancing on the westside, the phone rang and when my mother answered, a male voice growled, "Yor daughter's a nigger lover."

Cudjo Lynched

While the officers were looking for Cudjo, they met up with Ed Carolina, a negro who was drunk and showed fight. He was killed by some of the officers.
—*The Okemah Sledge Hammer*, (Socialist) 11/06/1913

Two of the friends I had danced with the night the phone call came bore the last name of Carolina, a family with deep roots in our part of Oklahoma. I don't know for sure, but I imagine they are related to Ed Carolina, who was killed by deputies during the Cudjo manhunt. I haven't asked, afraid I'll hurt my friends' feelings or open old wounds. I did ask a half-dozen of my male and female black childhood friends that I'm still in touch with if they'd heard of the Cudjo lynching. I wondered if it had been told in the black community as a cautionary tale. One of the friends I asked, whose mother was a Cudjo, said that the lynching was "a big family secret not talked about around the kids." Another said she'd heard of the lynching, but it wasn't talked about much.

Two others said they'd heard whispers of the Cudjo lynching and of others, but that there was no active oral transmission. "It's history," M.H. said, with a chorus of agreement from the rest, "and we're glad it's just history."

Another Lynching in Oklahoma
John Cudjo, the negro who killed Deputy Sheriff John Dennis in this county Saturday night was captured Tuesday afternoon, and brought to this city at about 8 o'clock when a mob seized him and hanged him to a telephone pole in front of the county court house. After the hanging at least one hundred shots were fired into the negro's body. The mob then dispersed very quietly and the town is quiet.

A large placard on which was written "To the Memory of Lee Cruce" was tied to the negro's feet as his body swung from the pole.
—*Tulsa Star*, African-American newspaper, 11/8/1913

Two Oklahoma lynchings, one following closely on the other, were used not only to satisfy the perpetrators' race hatred and thirst for vengeance, but also to send a political message. In both the November 1913 lynching of John Cudjo in Wewoka and the January 1914 lynching of Ben Dickerson in Noble, lynchers attached signs to the dead men's bodies that referenced the then governor of Oklahoma, Lee Cruce. Cudjo's sign, hung from twine around his ankles, read, "To the Memory of Lee Cruce." Dickerson's sign, hung around his neck, read, "If Lee Cruce wants to help this nigger out he will have to go to hell to do it." Governor Cruce was against capital punishment and had commuted the sentences of several legally tried and sentenced criminals.

Those who preferred lynchings to trials used Cruce's actions as a justification for lynching: if Cruce wouldn't apply the proper penalties, then the mob must. Some sources went so far as to blame Cruce for the increase in lynchings: "Persons who favor lynching declare that Governor Cruce's conscientious scruples against allowing any hangings during this term of office, his scruples against capital punishment, is the leading cause of so many lynchings in Oklahoma" (*Norman Transcript*, January 29, 1914). The human body, especially the female body and the body of color, has always been acted upon by the body politic—the anti-Cruce slogans made the politicization of the two men's bodies clearly evident.

In 2014, the Oklahoma legislature tried to outlaw the wearing of hoodies; the statute banned wearing a "robe, mask, or other disguise" in the public at any time; if passed, the bill would have become an "emergency" statute, immediately in force—supposedly, it was "immediately necessary for the preservation of the public peace, health and safety." When national public ridicule of the "hoodie law" began, some legislators tried to justify the bill by comparing it to Oklahoma Governor George Walton's 1923 law, still in effect, which prohibits concealing one's identity when committing a crime, a law specifically intended to make it easier to arrest and prosecute KKK members. Walton fought against the Klan from the moment he took office; he was impeached and removed from office a mere 11 months and 10 days after he was inaugurated.

Most liberal Oklahomans believe the 2014 bill was in reaction to the Summer of Ferguson. It failed.

University of Oklahoma Regent Thinks His City Once Had a More Superior Gene Pool
When I went on the school board 30... 25 years ago... a little over... we were, probably the best school district in the state. We

just happened to have the best gene pool. But that gene pool keeps moving out. It's moved to Edmond, it's now moved to Deer Creek, and ya know, they'll keep runnin' as long as they can buy green fields and gasoline for their car.
—*BlueNationReview.com*, 3/20/2015

When I was in graduate school at the University of Oklahoma, during a social event, I walked up to two women, both women of color whom I knew, and, reverting to the familiar way my friends and I spoke to each other just 40 miles east of the university, I said, "Hey, girl! Whassup? Watcha doin' for Thanksgiving?" One of the women was a professor in the English department; I was taking a class from her. Over the course of the semester, we had personality conflicts that led to accusations of misconduct on both sides. She told a faculty committee that I was a racist and had acted in a racist manner when I addressed her as "girl" at the social event. The accusation made me sick at my stomach. I had consciously attempted to rid myself of my upbringing, beginning when I was in elementary school. I hated my stepfather and I wanted to be whatever he didn't want me to be, hence, I did not want to be a racist. For as long as I could remember, I had enjoyed warm and egalitarian relationships with white kids, black kids, Indian kids, and the Laotian kid who moved to town when I was in fifth grade.

A year later, on the occasion of my 30th high school reunion, I was still unsettled by the racism accusation and the fact that it was incited by my use of a kinship term, a friendship term that also marked my working-class and regional roots. I asked my friends there, black, white, and Indian, if they thought of me as racist, and if so, to tell me how so I could fix it. A unanimous roar of laughter followed the question. There was also some hard teasing about me being just like I was in high school, "too damn serious." Then, together, we moved to the dance floor to memorialize Michael Jackson's recent death by doing the electric slide and a few moonwalks to a set of ten of his songs. But now, after researching and writing this essay and thinking about the incident with my professor over the last seven years, I have to check my privilege. My hurt feelings pale in comparison to the quotidian harassment that people of color endure. I must remember that folks who do not know me might be deeply disturbed by hearing certain charged words spoken by me in my southern accent, no matter how benignly I intend them, because they evoke a history I can neither change nor fully redeem by my own actions.

Unfortunately, racism is not relegated to Oklahoma's history.

Family Says Moore (OK) Police Beat Father To Death
Three Moore Police officers were put on administrative leave while detectives investigate an in-custody death from overnight. The family of the [black] man who died said police beat him badly and they recorded it with a cell phone camera.. [. . .] Lunahi Rodriguez said that five officers beat her father to death right in front of her, in the parking lot of the movie theater.
—*News9.com*, 2/15/2014

The years 2012-2014 were bad ones for race relations in America. Many of the names of victims of race-related violence are internationally recognizable: Trayvon Martin, Michael Brown, Eric Garner. Perhaps the murder of Luis Rodriguez in a Moore, Oklahoma, movie theater parking lot is less well known. Rodriguez was not accused of any crime; in fact, he was trying to deescalate a domestic spat between his wife and their daughter that took place in the theater parking lot. His wife, who appears to be white, slapped her daughter, and a bystander called police. Luis Rodriguez was trying to stop his upset wife from driving away when Moore police arrived. It appears they assumed he was responsible for the domestic disturbance and stopped him, demanding his ID. When Rodriguez attempted to continue across the parking lot to calm his wife, five officers took him down for not presenting identification when asked. They beat him with fists and knees and pepper-sprayed him. The officers ignored bystanders' (including the family's) insistence that he was not part of the disturbance; likewise, they turned a deaf ear to concerns for Rodriquez's well being. When officers finally handcuffed Rodriguez and turned him over (he had been face down), he was dead. And, as happened so often in the bad old days of Oklahoma lynchings, the officers were cleared of any wrongdoing and no one was indicted for the murder of Luis Rodriquez.

Neither was anyone indicted for the murder of Mary Nelson and her son; nor for the executions of John Cudjo and Henry Conley.

In Faulkner's story "Dry September," the motivations behind the lynching of innocent black man Will Mayes include race hatred and sheer meanness; the lynching is also figured as a sacrifice in response to drought. Like the body of John Cudjo which was made to serve as a political billboard, dead black bodies continue to serve their executioners as political statements and as sacrifices to exorcise national guilt and fear, as tribute to our increasingly authoritarian and militarized society, and as an outlet for individual violent tendencies. I wonder if no one knows the history of lynchings or if, as a society, we have truly decided that only certain lives matter. A dry-grass fire is raging across our country, one not of rumors but of hatred and anger. It's certain that if we keep going the direction we're going, Oklahomans and Americans, of all colors, will continue to live increasingly disfigured lives in an increasingly disfigured society. And all of our home-towns, all the Okemahs and Wewokas, will be hushed.

Notes

p. 17   This essay was originally written as the introduction to "Oklahoma Writing," a special issue of the online literary journal *Sugar Mule;* the special issue was later published in print form by my publishing company, Mongrel Empire Press. The resulting anthology, entitled *Ain't Nobody That Can Sing Like Me: New Oklahoma Writing,* is available through most online bookstores. Although I updated this essay in 2013, particularly the segments which list literary activities in Oklahoma, the majority of the content remains the same as when I wrote it in 2009. The online edition of "Oklahoma Writing" is still available at *SugarMule.com.*

p. 27   Originally published in *World Literature Today,* July/August 2013.

p.29   Versions of this review were published in the *Working-Class Studies Newsletter*; in those versions, the reviews were separated by author and shortened. This version was published on *This is Just to Say,* Oklahoma poet Benjamin Myers's blog, in October 2013.

p. 37   This essay was originally published in *Oklahoma Revelator* Issue 1 (Autumn 2008), a short-lived radical magazine edited by Rachel C. Jackson (Red Flag Press) with the assistance of Jeanetta Calhoun Mish (Mongrel Empire Press).

p. 37 "My People"   My friend Susan Kates sent me this poem after finding it in *Proud to be an Okie: Cultural Politics, Country Music, and Migration to Southern California* by Peter La Chapelle, U of California Press, 2007.

p. 41 ". . . outside of the usual country music suspects."
Books by people who DO know about Oklahoma music include: *Singing Cowboys and All That Jazz: A Short History of Popular Music in Oklahoma* by William W. Savage, U of OK Press, 1988; *From Blue Devils to Red Dirt: The Colors of Oklahoma Music* by John Wooley, Hawk Publishing Group, 2006; *Oklahoma Music Guide I & II: Biographies, Big Hits, and Annual Events*, New Forums Press, 2003, 2013; "Getting Along: Woody Guthrie and Oklahoma's Red Dirt Musicians" by Thomas Connor, published in *Alternative Oklahoma: Contrarian Views of the Sooner State,* U of OK Press, 2007.

p. 43 ". . . longtime Parman collaborator, Arn Henderson"
Arn has selflessly declined to mention that he coauthored, with Dortha Henderson, one of the essential documents on Oklahoma culture, *Architecture in Oklahoma: Landmark and Vernacular,* published by Parman's Point Riders Press in 1978.

p. 49 This essay was commissioned for and published in *Landscape Dreams: A New Mexico Portrait*, a collection of photographs by Craig Varjabedian. Copyright © 2012 University of New Mexico Press.

p. 61 Originally published in *World Literature Today*, Jan/Feb 2015.

p. 63 Originally published in *Oklahoma Today*, April/May 2014.

p. 71 Originally published in *Oklahoma Today* Sept/Oct 2013.

p. 75 Originally published in *Red Dirt Book Festival 2003 Anthology*. Norman, OK: Red Dirt Book Festival/Pioneer Library System, 2004. Republished in *Crosstimbers*, Fall/Winter 2008.

p. 83 Originally published in *Oklahoma Today*, March/April 2012.

p. 87 Originally published in *Sugar Mule Literary Magazine* 44, 8/15/2013.

p. 97 I'd like to extend my sincere gratitude to the Oklahoma Historical Society and the Oklahoma History Center; I could not have written this essay without their resources.

p. 102 Littlefield, 4

p. 104 Everett

Bibliography for "Culture Warriors," p. 37.

Butler, Ken. "A Night of Vengeance in Wewoka." *More Oklahoma Renegades*. Pelican Publishing, 2007. Print.

Census Bureau. *Census: Oklahoma*. Washington DC, USA: GPO, 1920. Print.

Clark Kicktode, Charles N. *Lynchings in Oklahoma: Vigilantism and Racism in the Twin Territories of Oklahoma, 1830-1930*. Shawnee, OK: Kicktode, 2008. Print.

Everett, Dianna. "Lynching," *Encyclopedia of Oklahoma History and Culture*, www.okhistory.org Web. 15 June 2015.

Goble, Danney. "The Ku Klux Kan in the 1920s." *Historical Atlas of Oklahoma*. 4th ed. Norman: U of OK P, 2006. Print.

Hayes, Terrence. "A Postcard from Okemah." *Ploughshares* 28.1 (2002): 66–68. Print.

Littlefield, Daniel F. *Seminole Burning: A Story of Racial Vengeance*. U Press of Mississippi, 1996. Print.

Loudenbeck, Doug. "Jim Crow in Oklahoma City." Blog. *Oklahoma City History Blog*. N.p., 1 May 2009. Web. 2 Apr. 2015.

McMahan, Anna. Interviewed by Grace Kelly, Oklahoma WPA. Indian Pioneer Collection, Oklahoma Historical Society. 1937.

Oklahoma Senate Bill 13. Don Barrington, author. 55th Oklahoma Legislature, 1st sess., January 2015.

Smith-Estrada, Carmen. "Oklahoma City African Americans Sit-in for Integration, 1958-64." Database. *Global Nonviolent Action Database.* n.p., 9 Dec. 2011. Web. 2 Mar. 2015.